HEART HEAD & HANDS

HEART, HEAD & HANDS

An Interpretation of Swedenborg's Writings
in relation to Psychological and Spiritual Well-Being

Stephen Russell-Lacy

SEMINAR BOOKS

LONDON

HEART, HEAD & HANDS
An Interpretation of Swedenborg's Writings
in relation to Psychological and Spiritual Well-Being

SEMINAR BOOKS   First Edition 2008

'Seminar Books' is an Imprint of The General Conference of the New Church
Registered Charity No. 253206, Swedenborg House, 20-21 Bloomsbury Way,
London. WC1A 2TH
Previously an Imprint of The Missionary Society of the New Church
Registered Charity No. 231408

ISBN 10 : 0-907295-36-3
ISBN 13 : 978-0-907295-36-5

British Library Cataloguing in Publication Data.
A catalogue record for this book is available from the British Library

Set in Baskerville 10/12 point

Typeset, printed and bound in Great Britain by
L.E.A. Printers, 49 Leesons Hill, Orpington, Kent. BR5 2LF

Designed by G.Roland Smith, MCSD, ACP.

Distributed by New Church House,
34 John Dalton Street, Manchester. M2 6LE
0161 834 4192
New Church College,
25 Radcliffe New Road, Radcliffe, Manchester. M26 1LE
0161 766 2521

Cover Picture : 'Chamber Music' by John Copley 1875-1950
Reproduced by kind permission of The Manchester City Art Gallery
and the copyright holder, Peter Copley

Contents

1 Introduction 7

2 Looking for Answers 12

3 Taking the Initiative 22

4 Valuing Sex 32

5 Working on Love 37

6 Being Acceptable 42

7 Gaining Self-Control 50

8 Finding Forgiveness 56

9 Calming Anger 64

10 Valuing what we Do 70

11 Facing our Flaws 74

12 Feeling Good about Oneself 81

13 Asking for Help 88

14 Learning to Trust 92

15 Attaining Peace of Mind 95

16 Dealing with Death 101

17 Surviving a Catastrophe 108

18 Coming to Terms with Voices 116

19 Shaking off Unhappy Moods 122

20 Reacting to Wrongdoers 128

21 Overcoming Obsessions 133

22 Discovering Confidence 137

23 Living through Crisis 145

24 Receiving Hope through Despair 150

25 Drawing Ideas Together 155

Chapter Notes 164

Selected Reading 170

More Swedenborgian Sources 174

Index 175

Acknowledgments

This book expands on the content of a series of leaflets produced for the Swedenborg Movement and I am grateful for the advice and encouragement of David Friend its Co-ordinator. I would also like to acknowledge my debt to the knowledge and understanding of my teachers, colleagues and students in the fields of clinical psychology and Swedenborgian teaching, particularly Michael Stanley for his time and knowledge in providing detailed comments, also David Lomax, David Gaffney, and Trevor Millar. I am grateful for the helpful feedback of friends and family including David Haseler, Edmund Preston, and my wife Carole and daughter Rachael. I thank Roland Smith for correcting the typescript and preparing it for printing. The quotations from world's religions are taken from 'Wisdom is One' edited and published by Andrew Dakers Limited London 1947.

Stephen Russell-Lacy December 2007

1. Introduction

Personal Problems

Everybody is in the same boat. We all have to face the challenge of the negative side of life. This may entail a feeling of unhappiness and a sense of being apart from other people and not really belonging. It may mean worry and unease about things going wrong and for some people it may mean great suffering. Alternatively, it may involve being puzzled about just being alive in the world. What is it all about then? Where do we come from and where are we going? In addition, perhaps more importantly, how do we deal with what life throws at us now?

Some of us learn from our anxiety, depression and anger and learn to deal with these emotional states. Others among us indulge them and allow our lives to be filled by them giving them the energy to harm us and others around us. What follows is my own attempt – as a cognitive-behavioural therapist and a student of Swedenborg's spiritual philosophy – to throw some light on how we can put these personal issues and emotional states into words and respond to them in a straightforward down-to-earth way. It is about what ideas we can consider that might give us a more positive perspective on life, and what things we can do to help us cope better with our lives and relationships. I hope this book will suit those who are interested in finding new ways of seeing life or who want to think about the choices that are open to them.

To this end I have drawn on some practical notions from modern psychological therapy. Sometimes just describing a problematic situation or a self-defeating way of thinking or behaving can lead to seeing a possible solution. More often however, whenever we spiral down in unhealthy thoughts, desires and actions, these all reinforce each other. Breaking the pattern requires much reflection and resolve. Nevertheless, it is possible to change negative habits of thought that adversely affect us. Once we bring such attitudes out into the open, we can examine them in the light of day and challenge them if unrealistic, and look to making some real changes in our attitudes and behaviour in relationships.

Holistic Approach – Heart, Head and Hands

These days it is widely recognised that, in dealing with personal problems, we need to help the whole person. The mind, the body and the spirit are considered together rather than focussing on any one of these in isolation. For example, it is advisable not only to allow a tired body sufficient rest, but also to provide conditions for a relaxed mind and time to be created for the reflection of the spirit. In other words, health-care, counselling and therapy professionals generally believe a holistic approach is necessary. This is the heart, head and hands of personal life – the emotional awareness of the heart, the ideas in the head, and the activity of the hands.

Personal Development

In what follows, I have linked some ideas from the fields of psychology and psychotherapy with those contained in the books of the eighteenth century visionary and spiritual philosopher, Emanuel Swedenborg [1]. This book is aimed at all who wish to understand how better to tackle the personal issues in life with which we are all challenged and in particular those who might be favourably inclined towards Swedenborg because of what they have heard or read of him as theologian, philosopher, scientist, or medium. I feel that more people may want to be made aware of the relevance of his system of thought concerning human spirituality and how this relates to, and can profoundly benefit, our individual lives. In this book I have endeavoured to couple my own interpretation of his psychospiritual writings with the modern psychology of personal well-being and individual development. Like many modern transpersonal psychologists, I believe spiritual teachings deepen and enrich psychological ideas, and that the latter can help to put the flesh on the bones of the former.

A major point of interest is the topic of personal *development* – one that goes beyond a concern with simply the psychological well-being of the individual. So, for example, this book looks at how we can deal with the anger, depression and anxiety that form part of milder emotional disorders in a way that can enhance our inner growth.

Correspondence of Inner and Outer

Swedenborg's spiritual ideas have often been associated either with the paranormal or with religion and thus do not appear to fit in easily with the prevalent belief in Western culture that it is only the things that scientists can examine that can possibly provide the answers to our questions about the world in which we live. It is difficult enough to find scientific evidence for the clairvoyant claims of psychics let alone for the existence of God. It is much easier to research into what can be observed, for example plant cells and rock formations. On the other hand, spiritual teachers throughout history have encouraged us to focus more on the inner things of the heart and mind. In this way, the external problems of life should affect our inner life less negatively.

"He whose soul is not attached to external objects
obtains the happiness that is in one's self."
(Krishna. *Bhagavad-Gita*, v, 21 – Hindu tradition)

"The wise man is concerned with inner things,
he is not concerned with outer things."
(Lao Tse. *Tao Teb King*, xii. – Taoist tradition)

In directing attention towards the inner life of the soul, Swedenborg talks of a correspondence that exists between inner and outer things[2].

We recognise someone's inner feeling by observing the outer expressions on their face. A smile, frown or glare is a physical change in the facial muscles that is a sign of the inner state of the person – unless he or she happens to be a skilled actor or a hypocrite! Likewise, a beckoning motion of the hands and arms can convey a welcoming attitude. A soothing or harsh tone of voice conveys kindness or anger.

We find it easier to speak explicitly about inner things in terms of outer ones. For example when we refer to vision, we mean understanding – as in 'I see what you mean', or 'the light is dawning'. When we talk of the heart, we mean feeling – as in 'hard-hearted', 'broken-hearted'.

As adults, we do not much use the language of our private inner world except perhaps in intimate disclosure with a close friend or when talking with our therapist or when discussing a novel. At other times such matters may enter dialogue only tangentially as we focus on the practical aspects of earning a living, getting on with other people and managing our financial and domestic life.

Although psychologists are interested in how we talk about the physical things we see in the world about us, they also study non-literal aspects of language where things referred to are not as they seem; where the full meaning cannot be comprehended from the literal sense. Young children are known to take a literal view of things, not understanding the frequent metaphor and irony used by adults. Sarcasm is another example of a linguistic form that requires our re-interpretation as in 'That was a brilliant thing to do', said of an obviously stupid action. Another example is hyperbole, as when we say 'There are millions of people in our office' suggesting there are many people we have to get along with at work but clearly not millions. In line with this work is the study of the way people speak using one word or phrase to represent another.

Metaphors have been called 'double-aspect' terms [3] because they have connected meanings in both the material and the inner personal domains. To illustrate, we apply the word 'strength' both to physical strength and to strength of character. The world of nature can be seen to reflect the mind's inner appreciation of life. For example:

- Flowers echo the tender loving thoughts that are so beautiful while they last.

- A storm with torrential rain and hail reflects what is fierce and cruel.

We can learn much about the human spirit by watching what nature is teaching us.

"As above, so below; as below, so above"
(Sayings of the medieval alchemists)

Swedenborgian Psychology

Swedenborg has not as yet been widely recognised as an important source of psychological ideas. One reason is probably because his books were published in the 18th century in Latin and even in modern English translation they are not easily readable. Yet I believe they contain many startling thoughts regarding a dimension to life that often we miss, being caught up, as we are, in so many of the illusory appearances of the world around us. One example concerns the way our dreams express unconscious creative and destructive impulses that inwardly motivate us. He wrote about this over a hundred years before Sigmund Freud who, in exploring the symbolism of dreams, declared that dreams are the "the royal road to the unconscious."

For me, Swedenborg's writings often have a distinctly practical psychological stance. This may sound surprising to those who know him more as an intellectual writer. However, this practicality is evident in so far as he deals with a psycho-spiritual dimension to life. For he is

10

concerned not only with the inclinations of human nature, and the factors that motivate us but also with such subjects as individual personal growth, the inner aspects of the sexual relationship, human rationality and inner liberty. I hope this introduction to some of his ideas will suggest their relevance to the topics covered as well as to their application for our individual mental health and well-being.

In most chapters, I have tried to provide material from the field of cognitive-behavioural psychotherapy. This type of psychotherapy focuses on teaching how to examine, challenge, and replace those self-defeating habits of thought and behaviour that maintain an individual's emotional or relationship problems. I then attempt also to link psycho-spiritual teachings gleaned from Swedenborg with each topic; the final chapter drawing his ideas together.

When I started to write this book I thought I was writing about things from the human perspective. It was to be more a book of psychology than theology. I know many people have been put off religion and so I wanted to show the relevance of the spiritual to the personal side of our lives. However, I discovered it was nigh impossible for me not to give a lot of mention to the divine creative source. Try as I might, I just could not leave out God from the picture. Perhaps this should not have surprised me, but it did. I suppose the result reflects my own basic faith and convictions and someone with a different background would have produced a different emphasis.

At the end of the book, there is a section of Chapter Notes containing suggested further reading relevant to each chapter. For example, in the chapter notes for this Introduction, I have listed a number of biographies for those readers who might be interested in the many-facetted life of Swedenborg the man.

2. Looking for Answers

From our childhood onwards our lives are filled with questions of one sort or another – some more pressing or even agonising than others. But where are we to – or should we – look for valid answers?

Asking Big Questions

There are the really big questions and the smaller ones. Here are a few of the bigger ones. Does outer space beyond our solar system go on forever or does it have an edge – and if so what is on the other side? Where do we come from, why are we here, and what will become of us when we die? I can imagine some alien intelligence on a far distant planet asking exactly the same questions. These sorts of universal questions have puzzled thinking people down the ages.

Children as well as adults ask questions. The play-age stage of childhood is often characterised by developmental theorists as one of explorative activity and exuberant discovery. Consequently good educational practice encourages a child-centred approach to learning. This compares favourably with the old approach of rote learning. Modern teachers enhance children's interest by providing knowledge, building on what they already know. They relate their teaching to the child's limited experiences stretching their understanding a bit further.

Young children's concrete thinking and love of knowing things seems to go deeper than mere curiosity about the physical things they see. When Argentina invaded the Falkland Islands in 1982, the then Superintendent of Education said his three year-old daughter asked all sorts of difficult questions. After watching groups of morose Argentine soldiers being led up into the hills, she would ask "Are they bad men, Daddy?" He would say, "No, of course they're not bad men. Some of them are probably very good men, but what they're doing isn't very nice." To which she replied "So why doesn't anybody like them, then?"

There may be naïvety in their outlook but there is also a simple interest in asking for basic reasons for things. They can even ask astonishingly deep and perceptive questions albeit in their childlike way:

"Why can't we see God?"

"Why does God let us get hurt when we are good?"

"Why did God make rats?"

Unfortunately they do not often get satisfactory answers.

When growing up we may have become frustrated trying to get answers – so much so that we gave up asking about anything really important. If you do not get a meaningful response to your query, then you tend to stop asking and the issue eventually disappears from your conscious mind. This can happen sometimes if parents give no reasons when responding to children e.g. saying "So and so is true because I say so". Alternatively, parents may, more or less, restate the question using different words e.g. "Why is that man acting so crazy?" "Because he's insane."

On the other hand there are helpful parents and teachers who may have heard what Albert Einstein once said:

"Don't take no for an answer.
The important thing is never to stop questioning."

These days the age of religious dogma has begun to pass away and we expect to think about things in a rational way. We can grasp ideas according to what others tell us. For example, we can learn about ideas in philosophy and other fields of thought. Yet, mere knowledge is not enough for a proper understanding.

People who follow Einstein's advice tend to encourage questioning. This could be by using brainstorming. For example, "Why are some people gay?" "Maybe it is inborn, maybe personal choice or maybe something to do with what happens to the individual." When brainstorming, it is important to remember to put all ideas on the table. Decide later, which ones to toss into the rubbish bin. The enquiring mind can then be encouraged to consider alternative explanations and a means of evaluating them. "What are the arguments for and against each viewpoint?" "What sort of information will help us evaluate each one?" "Where would we find this information?"

The teacher can help younger school pupils to find things out using children's love of knowledge. He or she can take advantage of their interest to provide straightforward facts and simple explanations that may be suited to those with a limited experience of life.

However, when they get older these children need their teacher to give them the ways and means of finding out answers for themselves – how to use a library, what books to consult or what considerations to bear in mind. In this way, they can form their own ideas and make their own conclusions. It is the same for all of us. In the end, we will not find the answers to life's quandaries just in what others tell us. Neither will the language of everyday conversation, soap-opera scripts, newspaper news, business discussion, or scientific endeavour do more than tangentially touch what we need to understand. More meaningful answers to life's big questions coming from inner experience can start to suggest themselves however during intimate conversation between close friends, in the lines of the poet and in the private prayers of the sincere at heart. In addition, the writing of spiritual teachers and sacred scriptures of the world's religions directly address them.

Looking Within

It is when we look within that we have a chance of illumination. We can be very knowledgeable for example about the ideas of Mahatma Gandhi, C.G. Jung or Karl Marx or whatever system of thought that appeals. We do need to use our heads to make sense of things we hear and see around us. Genuine enlightenment, however, never came just from listening to a lecture or reading a book – even this one! It also comes from within and not just from without. It is holistic – not just a memory and intellectual understanding of what somebody else has written or said – but also from our feeling, and the effort in what we do. In other words, it is something involving our whole being – heart, head and hands.

Put another way our soul, mind and body are all involved. Many people may reject fundamentalist religious dogma but want to learn more about the spiritual side of life. They realise that there is more to life than the evidence of science. That one needs to look deep within the spirit of things to discover answers to our personal questions. Knowledge based on the world of nature and gained through our senses is limited.

"Are not all your ideas borrowed from your senses,
which do not give you the reality but only its phenomena? …
For absolute truth is not to be found in the phenomenal world"
(Eckartshausen. *The Cloud upon the Sanctuary*, i. – Roman Catholic mystic)

The talking therapies help us to focus on an inner realm of emotion and desire, imagination and intuition, thought and belief, of which we had been largely unconscious. Spiritual exercises such as prayer, meditation and contemplation reveal even more depth of mind. They can pry us away from ordinary desires and connect us with a deeper will and purpose. When we practice meditation, we try to focus our attention and suspend judgment whilst maintaining objectivity. This means passively observing thoughts and feelings simply as mental events without personal attachment to them. In this way with repeated practice, we still the mind and distance ourselves from our thoughts and feelings that we can then calmly examine. As a child, Swedenborg was able to concentrate intensely on an idea with a slowing of breathing. He later differentiated, on the one hand, this meditation from, on the other, thought of the body, imagination and daydreaming.

We can extend our experience of meditation exercises to a general mindfulness attitude throughout our daily life. Mindfulness is focusing our attention on one thing at a time, engaging our mind with what we see or hear. This would mean, for example, paying close attention to what a friend is saying, the tone of voice, the facial expression, the bodily posture and orientation and so on. Not allowing ourselves to be distracted by a hundred and one thoughts that flash into the mind but really listening to what is being said with no wandering attention. This is an attitude of acknowledging and facing our experience of the friend instead of fighting the experience or trying to make it something else. In addition, it means dealing with the immediacy of the current situation, rather than a possible future or the past; what we might call focusing on the 'eternal now'.

The soul of life is more than what can be seen with the eyes, heard with the ears, or touched with the skin despite what those with a worldly orientation might claim. The spirit of the age may have been lost but perhaps we can find it again. Not all religion is fanatical or a banal theory without relevance to the real hardships of life. There are actually answers to our questions which we could find within the deeper levels of our being that might possibly lead us out of our troubles.

"The Spirit of truth. The world cannot accept him, because it neither sees him nor knows him. But you know him, for he lives with you and will be in you."
(John 14:17)

Feelings of our Heart

We may voice a viewpoint to others around us because this is convenient for us rather than because it is right. For example, we may take on board and give voice to the opinions of other people, whether realistic or mistaken, so that they can better like us and find us socially acceptable. Yet, as has been said:

"If a million people say a foolish thing, it is still a foolish thing."
(Jacques Anatole Thibault)

Conventional opinion that fails to address contradictions and lack of evidence does not put off those searching for the correct answer.

What is it that we want? Do we want the truth? Existential writers often speak of our search for meaning; the meaning to each of us of a shared calamity, a celebration or a milestone reached and passed. One person might be keen to find a comfortable understanding rather than finding out how things really are. Another may want to impose his or her own solutions based on a favourite hobbyhorse or particular prejudice. The trouble is that self-interest and pride get in the way of light illuminating the human mind. I would say that part of the route to enlightenment is a heart-felt interest in what is true, for its own sake, rather than for any advantage it can give us.

We might want to find out an answer to a problem for the sake of what is good and useful in the answer. We are less likely to learn how to repair a punctured bicycle tyre until we become interested in cycling. We may not understand our child's difficulty at school unless we really want to make his or her life happy. The answer to the question of what job to apply for may not appear until we have an inkling of what we want to do.

We also need to look deeply into our inner being if we want to find answers to the really weighty questions. Soulful music is full of deep feeling and profoundly moving. It expresses a self-reflection that reaches down beyond the superficialities of life and the sentiments that too easily arise from our moods, to a more considered feeling about the human predicament. Unless we engage our deeper emotions in our search, we cannot expect to arrive at meaningful answers to our questions.

Thoughts of our Head.

To use one's intelligence does not mean one has to be academically intellectual. Coming from somewhere within is a light that illuminates. It enables us to think clearly, to see the ramifications, to weigh up the pros and cons and to understand the reasons for things. Unless we use the understanding in our heads, what we conclude may be irrational and unrealistic.

Effort of our Hands

Our hands also come into the picture; what we actually do. We need to make the effort to do things, to find solutions. To find answers to their questions scientists do experiments. We also need to do things. If our question is the simple one about repairing a bicycle wheel then this would mean our removing the wheel, separating the inner tube from the tyre, locating the hole, sticking a patch and replacing everything properly. Only when we do it will we have the answer we need. Practice makes perfect.

However, to get answers to bigger questions we could go to the library, look on the internet, or telephone someone to ask a question. If the answer sought is to do with our child's problem we could go to his or her school, find the right teacher, and initiate a conversation to discuss the child's problem. We need to read the appropriate newspaper or journal, seek out a relevant job advert, and send off for details.

Psychological therapists can only comment on what a client chooses to reveal about him or herself. If the client does not share enough of the story about him or herself to work on, the therapist may be ineffective. Real self-insight comes only from the client actually disclosing information and inner feelings despite the discomfort this often causes; making the effort to get beyond the usual comfortable excuses and self-justifications. This is the therapeutic work necessary for personal improvement. The more we put into something then the more we get out of it. We speak of creativity - for example producing a finished piece of music or sculpture - as involving one percent inspiration but ninety-nine percent perspiration. The effort the sculptor or musician makes to find answers to the artistic problem is crucial if the answers are to appear.

To conclude we cannot really get answers unless we have the relevant information concerning what is true, want to see what is good in it and actually do something to find out.

Illusion and Reality

Propaganda does not respect the truth and so it is said that the truth is the first victim in the fog of war. Pontius Pilate once asked Christ, "What is truth?" In considering the idea of truth, we can distinguish between illusion and reality. It appears that the sun revolves around the earth whereas actually the earth goes round the sun.

It appears that showing respect to friends and acquaintances and giving generously to charitable organisations is a sign of a true social conscience. However, this is an illusion in the case of those manipulating the good opinion of others by hypocritical pretence.

Some people fall for the illusions of time. As the saying goes: "Yesterday has gone; tomorrow is a post-dated cheque, today is cash." By focusing on the present moment, we can be more fully involved with what is deeply true about life. Writers influenced by Eastern world spirituality describe ordinary consciousness in terms of an incessant mental noise arising from our entanglement with what has been going on for us in the world. This level of mind attaches itself to space and time and is said to hinder our awareness of a realm of stillness. However, as I mentioned above, we could find a deeper self and an enlightened state of consciousness when we start to focus on the 'eternal now' instead of living in the past and worrying about the future – a state of consciousness, free of the burden of time.

Another example of an illusion is the idea that the happiest people are those who give priority to pleasure and personal gain. I believe actually the happiest among us are those whose main concern is the well-being of others. This is the true heavenly state. For the state of heaven can be within us.

"In the space within the heart are contained both heaven and earth"
(Chandogya *Upanishad*, viii, I, 3. – Hindu tradition)

"Nor will people say, 'Here it is,' or 'There it is,'
because the kingdom of God is within you."
(Luke 17:21)

We can pretend we are in a heavenly state and we can deny and not face up to our failings. Then we are living a lie. Instead, we could start to resist our personal demons and work on our inner problems. Then we would more clearly see the reality within and around us rather than the illusions that were previously misleading us.

These examples show that the assumptions behind our questioning can be either illusory or realistic.

Inspiration of Illumination

When it comes down to it, I would suggest that only inspiration could illuminate our minds. But where does inspiration come from? In one sense, the word means the inhalation of air into the lungs; not that we can claim any credit for that as we usually breathe automatically without any conscious thought. However it is possible to learn to slow down one's breathing and the resulting change in the oxygen / carbon dioxide balance in the blood is thought to affect the brain and allow awareness of inner thoughts. Eastern yogis practise breath control to facilitate a state of deep absorption and concentration during meditation. Likewise, as pointed out before, Swedenborg himself reported, since childhood, being better able to keep his mind fixed on a central thought by hardly breathing.

The word 'inspiration' also means stimulation of the mind inducing a high level of activity. The bored and apathetic individual uninvolved with life lacks stimulation of mind and consequently cannot clearly see the way forward. He or she is groping around in the dark. However, the mystic has often said that if we wish to see the way forward we can listen to an Inner Teacher to inspire our understanding and illuminate our path. This is to do with a further aspect of inspiration i.e. what many regard as divine guidance or influence exerted directly on the mind.

The novelist Leo Tolstoy grappled with his quest for a meaningful truth about life.[1] He remembered one day in early spring when alone in the forest, listening to its mysterious noises. His thought went back to that with which he had always been busy – looking for answers about the spirit of the divine within the universe. He was wondering how he ever came by the idea of God. There then arose within him a something that he called a 'glad aspiration towards life'. Everything in him woke up and received a meaning. A silent voice within him asked why he was looking any further for 'God is here, without whom one cannot live'. After realising that there is no existence without God, he says things cleared up both within and around him and the light never wholly died away. It saved him from suicide. His energy for living returned. His sole purpose became one of being a better person. He gave up the ways of the conventional world with its superfluities embracing instead the life of the peasants and felt relatively right and happy after this.

Like Tolstoy, when we search for true meaning we may also become aware of an inner light. It is amazing what some busy people can achieve. The more effort they put into what they do then the more understanding and inspiration they seem to have.

Spiritual Awareness

In considering our search for answers to questions, I have stated several factors. However, I believe it boils down to whether we think from a worldly or from a spiritual perspective. Scientists and many others in the academic world would be the first to say that they are not approaching their questions from a spiritual perspective. These thinkers believe nothing without facts of scholarship or research findings as evidence. They insist on answers that appear logical to them. They are constantly coming up with arguments against any ideas of a spiritual nature.

On the other hand spiritual thinkers trust in the divine. They say that what rational considerations they hear, and what things of nature they see, all combine to confirm their basic attitude. One example of this is the idea that hearing conversation does not belong to the ears but to the spirit that hears the meaning of what people say. Actually, Swedenborg's spiritual teachings tend to appeal to my rational thinking. I do not find his works to be illogical as many suppose the writings of mysticism and religion to be.

Those searching for answers to the big questions, who have a love of the spiritual, have recognised an underlying order around them – shown, for example, in the laws of physics. They have realised that no-one can explain away, as a series of accidents, the amazing universe of planets and stars, or the pattern of evolution on earth . They have seen more clearly and in a deeper way what others have said or written. The upshot has often been seeing life, more and more in a spiritual way, as created by a purposeful intelligence.

They had always been aware that the human body can give meaningful expression to inner thoughts and feelings; for example a welcoming standpoint through a beckoning gesture of the hands, a feeling of delight by a smiling facial expression, and an attitude of kindness by a soothing tone of voice. However, once they adopt a mental set of seeing the world in psycho-spiritual terms, they more clearly perceive how outward things around them reflect inward human qualities. They become more sensitive to what nature can teach. Now they begin to see how the things in the natural world reflect so many emotions and activities of the mind.

I believe it is possible to gain from the world of nature an appreciation of spiritual things: but I think to do so requires an interest of the heart regarding what is deeply and inwardly good and true in life. It means following the advice offered by Jesus.

"Ask and it will be given to you; seek and you will find; knock and the door will be opened to you."
(Matthew 7:7)

Our hands, heart and head can work in unison. We can find out things without easily being put off. We can value the good in what has been offered. We do not necessarily accept blindly what we have been told but can rather ponder over it in a reasonable way. Finally, we can hopefully become more sensitive to what nature can teach us about the reality of the psycho-spiritual side of life.

Spiritual illumination comes from loving what is good in the truth about some human situation and living it.[2]

"When a person is governed by what is good, it is from that good that he sees truths, perceives them, and so believes that they are indeed truths … what is good is like a little flame which sheds light and provides illumination, and so enables a person to see, perceive, and believe truths."
(Swedenborg. *Arcana Coelestia* section 5816[2])

3. Taking the Initiative

Often and in various ways we may slide into letting life around us govern how we think and behave – in a way that enables us to blame 'it' if ever we feel criticised. So it's always "someone else's fault – not mine!".

Our False Self

Some of us are naturally thoughtful and generous. We are willing to be of help to others even when it is an inconvenience. It is good to be selfless and charitable. However, do we sometimes allow others to exploit our better nature? One sign of this is if we were to feel fed up with the way others take advantage of us or feel quietly resentful when sidelined, or put on.

It is not necessarily the fault of the other person. We may be adding to our troubles by the way we regularly give in to what someone wants. At times perhaps acting like a doormat for them to wipe their feet on. Like when we find ourselves meekly submitting to what our family and friends demand; limply agreeing to go where someone asks us to go and doing whatever they suggest. We do not have a sense of our true selves because we are too busy meeting others expectations. Without thinking we fall in with what they say.

Adolf Hitler once said:

"What luck for the rulers that men do not think."

Why would anyone be so daft as constantly to do things that another person wants instead of thinking through their own views? It may be because we value ourselves less than we value others. This might show in conversation: "I'm sure you're right." "I'll leave that up to you." Some of us believe ourselves to be happy if we relate to others in this way but without our realising there is an inner assumption that what we want does not count, or that we do not really matter. Thinking so little of ourselves, the idea that we have any choice does not occur to us; in other words, we are tamely trying to please for fear of someone disliking us. We keep striving for the unobtainable, not realising that we can never gain everybody's approval.

Inner Freedom

Just as we may need to be less passive with other people, so we also may need to learn to take the initiative in relation to ourselves. Having a healthy relationship with others also means having a healthy relationship with oneself. Some people drift aimlessly through life reacting to events and never making things happen for themselves. However, whatever the personal problem, it is often necessary for us to take the initiative in doing something about it, rather than letting things drift. Otherwise, it is only when some crisis occurs that eventually the situation forces us to make decisions about say a job, home, or even a close relationship. Better to prevent difficulties getting out of hand than allow circumstances no longer under our control to push us into a corner.

In psychotherapy it is generally accepted that if patients persist in blaming some other person or thing for their problems of living, then no real therapy is possible. A therapist may ask such an individual, whose partner keeps running him or her down, or using violence, why not do something about it like insisting on a trial separation to bring the other person to their senses? In not accepting the responsibility for the way they live their lives, they cannot start to take hold of their own self and destiny. Thus for such people any personal growth is delayed.

The trouble is that many people are told that they are not at liberty to change their ways and that human freedom is questionable. For example, psychoanalysis – a branch of psychotherapy that follows the writings of Sigmund Freud – says we are not free because we are unaware of our unconscious complexes. Moreover, many behaviourists argue that our freedom is illusory because we are conditioned by the world around us e.g. the rewards and punishments in the family or the workplace, that shape our attitudes and life choices.

There is some – albeit limited – truth in these viewpoints. None of us is free to change our inherited disposition and the home environment when we are young. Because of differences in, for example, types of temperament and parental attitudes, we need individually to travel on our own unique spiritual journey. How the individual develops will be limited according to his or her makeup and life circumstances. We start at different places. The rôle models to whom we happen to be exposed affect how we mature.

Nature and nurture will both influence our development and affect in what ways we need to change, and the opportunities for so doing. They will affect what lessons in life we may learn. You cannot so easily learn French without a foreign language teacher. However, you do not need special learning if French is your native tongue. In one sense, the whole of the explanatory findings of psychology, studied as a science, demonstrate the restrictions on, and handicaps to, our individual freedom. These could be for example:

- Our beliefs and attitudes acquired, conforming to the cultural norms of home and society

- Our levels of self-esteem and self-confidence, due to the behaviour of others

- Our levels of talent and ability, emotional stability and physical strength, due to inherited constitution.

Our social, financial and physical circumstances affect the opportunities around us for personal growth. According to the situations they find themselves in, people vary in what they are obliged to do and thus what social rôles others expect of them. The need for earned income, family home-making, care for sick and elderly, supervision of children, etc. will vary from one person and circumstance to another.

These are clear physical, economic, legal, social and moral limits as well as psychological restrictions on our freedom to do certain things and act in certain ways. There may be very real boundaries to what we can do in any set of circumstances.

Despite all these factors apparently determining our behaviour, we actually feel individually free to choose what we do and make up our own minds about things – including whether to believe that we are free to make up our own minds! In other words, we all tend to believe in our own free will.

Isaac Bashevis Singer once said:

"You must believe in free will; there is no choice"

This may seem like a paradox! However, unless we are free to reflect on things, our thinking would lack any discernment. Many people recognize that being human, we do have many private choices in life; whether to try to read this book,or give up thinking about what it says;

whether to go along with the crowd or to do our own thing; whether to choose worldly or spiritual values. We may make decisions using so-called 'enlightened self-interest' or alternatively ethical ideas like what is fair or sincere. We can choose to travel on one road or on another.

"No one can serve two masters. Either he will hate the one and love the other, or he will be devoted to the one and despise the other. You cannot serve both God and Money."
(Matthew 6:24)

"One is the road to wealth, another the road that leads to Nirvana."
(*Dhammapada*, 75. Buddhist tradition)

Psychotherapists who take an existential approach to therapy tend to believe that whatever the particular types of theoretical formulation, techniques employed and therapist's personal style of conducting treatment, the client will only benefit if the therapy also influences the person's will. The therapist can neither create nor infuse the individual with a new will, but the therapist can help the patient to liberate will – to remove encumbrances from the bound, stifled will.

Although our choices may sometimes need to remain hidden until outward circumstances change, inwardly we are in a state of balance between, for example, optimism and pessimism or honesty and self-deception, Which we turn to is our own choice.

Swedenborg's view is that this balance is a state of equilibrium between good and bad influences on us from inside our minds. We have the option of directing ourselves towards higher or lower things. By deciding between two different ideas, or plans of action, we express our essential awareness of ourselves as an individual. [1]

Yet, in so far as some of our attitudes are unconscious or conditioned, then we are not free to tackle them. With increasing frequency, patients seek professional help with vague, ill-defined complaints. A first session may be finished with no clear picture of the patient's problem. The fact that the patient cannot define the problem is the actual problem.

Psychotherapy and personal counselling can help throw light on these hidden processes. For example, the overweight person may feel anxious about leaving food on the plate because of parental disapproval concerning waste when the individual was a child. Arguably, clearer self-insight actually increases our inner freedom.

And in my experience if I asked patients about the aspects of therapy that they found particularly useful, they often cite the discovery and assumption of personal responsibility. However, readiness to accept responsibility varies considerably. For some individuals it is extraordinarily difficult and this issue is the main task of psychotherapy; once they assume responsibility, therapeutic change almost happens automatically without much further effort for the therapist.

Rationality and Freedom

I am suggesting we each have two spiritual faculties, which make us human. The first of these is the ability to think for ourselves; being able to see things in a rational way from a higher perspective. This could mean, for example, seeing some family squabble in a rational way without one side or the other unduly swaying us emotionally.

With reasoning comes increased freedom – the second faculty. Only when we are able to see things from a rational perspective do we become free to choose between more than one viewpoint.

It is when we appreciate what a newspaper article is really about, that we can then freely choose whether to read it to the end. We use our head to think about what the writer is saying and our hands to turn the pages. However, we also need a heartfelt interest in the truth about the subject if we are really to learn anything from the printed words. Otherwise, our response to it is just going through the motions based on a reflex habit. Then we may go to the shop, buy the newspaper and return home, settling down in the chair and reading whatever is written because this is what we do everyday.

Likewise, only when we really think about the consequences of a crowd's behaviour, can we then freely decide whether to join in. The emotion of the moment may capture us. Everybody is shouting the same thing and focusing their attention on the same place. Therefore, we feel ourselves drawn to conform to what everybody is doing and saying. Yet, we are rational human beings. We can transcend the social pressure by using our ability to think about what is right in the situation. Is the crowd doing something in accord with what we value? What is the truth of the matter? In other words, as Christ says "the truth will set you free." Otherwise, we are simply reacting to the pressure of habit or social conformity.

Humanistic psychology is an approach in psychology that focuses on how people fulfil their individual potentials as a way of overcoming personal problems. Human freedom is said to be real, and must be consciously acknowledged, exercised and experienced for any authentic human existence. In other words a person, within certain limits, may become whatever he wills to become. We can all choose to develop any aspect of our makeup that we please. The explorer has opted to develop his or her curiosity and adventurous spirit. Couples, in deciding on parenthood, have decided to focus on their caring and nurturing side. Conscientious objectors and protestors have chosen to act on principles and ideals learned in youth despite the risks involved. To my way of thinking, the opening up of the higher mind widens our inner freedom. This means seeing things from a higher perspective and acting on these insights. Until this happens, I would argue, we will simply follow our natural tendencies and conditioning along the lines the psychoanalysts and behaviourists have indicated.

We can also point to the importance of wise teaching by parents in the formation of the higher mind in the child. They brought us up with good ideas that initially develop this level of mind. The spiritually-minded think of those early beginnings as the foundation for the building of conscience – through which an inner light can allow us to see when we are going wrong. I believe it is divinely inspired into the hearts and minds of those who want to follow what is right and good.

This occurs, for instance, when we believe that people should keep to the civil and criminal law because it is based on principles of justice and social order. Another example is the belief that doctors, architects and other occupational groups should follow their codes of practice and professional ethics because these derive from the value of high standards of work done for the benefit of clients. Essentially a true conscience includes a caring attitude to others, tolerance of their imperfections and following what is right in life.

I believe a higher self within us is our link with the bright light of divine inspiration. This is the source of our understanding of rational considerations and spiritual principles. These create new horizons and new ways forward. All of us can actually hope to achieve this. If we do not pursue this path, our bodily-centred illusions will limit us. Such an illusion for example is the fallacy that the route to happiness is to 'eat, drink and be merry'. Actually, experience teaches us that such activities, of themselves, can bring no lasting contentment beyond the pleasure of the moment. Life also consists of things of the spirit – such as quality time with others or the deeper satisfaction that comes from being part of useful activity. Bodily-centred illusions come from the mere appearance of things according to the senses of the body uninspired by higher meaning.

Playing Life's Cards

As we gain a reasonable appreciation of our own character, we then become free to choose to leave behind our personal hang-ups and instead develop our natural talents and personal potential. Such self-insight usually happens in counselling and psychotherapy.

A form of psychotherapy known as Reality Therapy [2], assumes that people develop psychiatric problems because of an inability to fulfil their needs and that fulfilling needs means taking on an attitude of responsibility for others as well as self. If a cure is to be effected the patient must be involved with other people or at least with one other person. Therefore, one cannot completely lock up oneself in oneself and one's own needs if therapy is to make any progress.

Yet, most of us do not need professional help. We can all choose to make better use of the opportunities that life presents to us. The more we put into the things we do, the more we are likely to get back – whether it is an occupational training course, a friendship, or a business.

Personal responsibility comes from our freedom to react to what life throws at us in the way we choose. In other words, it is not the hand of cards that life deals us that determine our destiny but rather the way we play those cards. We are responsible for whether we take hold of life or not.

A man sat in a bar in New York. [3] He was homeless, friendless and penniless having pawned or sold everything he owned for alcohol. He had not eaten for four days. He sat there thinking. He had often said that he would never let himself be cornered, and when the time came, he would find a home at the bottom of the river. However, he was too ill to walk even a quarter of the way to the river. As he sat there thinking, he seemed to feel some uplifting presence. He did not know what it was. He walked up to the bar and pounded it with his fist making the glasses rattle. Those who stood by drinking looked on with scornful curiosity. He said he would never take another drink. However, the thought immediately came that if he wanted to keep this promise he had better go and get himself locked up. Therefore, that is exactly what he did. He went to the nearest police station and the officer placed him in a narrow cell. He said it seemed as though all the demons that could find room came in that place with him. However, he prayed to his God and, although he did not feel any great help, carried on praying. When finally released he found his way to his brother's house where he was looked after. The next day he went to a local outdoor religious meeting and with great difficulty made his way to the space near the platform. There was a huge conflict going on within him but as he listened to the testimony of other alcoholics, he made up his mind that he would grasp the nettle and completely give up drink with help from a higher power. He promised God that if he were to take away his appetite for strong drink he would work for him all his life. The man's name was S. H. Hadley who became an active and useful helper of alcoholics in America.

Taking the Bull by the Horns

Not all of us get ourselves into such dire straights but at some point in our lives, we all need to change something important. Human nature being what it is – a mixture of positive and negative traits – there are things in all of us that we need to face up to: the bad habits, attitudes and desires that we have confirmed in our daily living for which we are culpable. For no-one else has chosen to remain in our negative pattern of behaviour. These elements of our heart, head and hands need reversing if we are to grow in maturity and spirituality. It is not enough to acknowledge our difficulties and opportunities; not sufficient to see things in rational light. We also need to accept in our hearts that personal amendment is necessary if we are to find personal growth. This means paying attention to the issues and making a conscious effort with clear intention to change.

In other words, an act of will freely made is required. The spirit of truth will hold us responsible for how we act. When we better understand the problems we are causing ourselves and our families, we may then either do nothing about it or we may actually then resolve to change, for example, our addiction to work, our avoidance of some personal issue or our emotional dependence on some particular person etc. We need to make a decision to take hold of our life rather than drift on as before. If psychotherapy is about anything, it is about personal change. The same goes for religious affiliation. It applies to all of us. It means acknowledging the truth about something, resolving to do something about it and then acting. Our destiny is in our own hands - whether we stay sober, put our financial affairs into good order, are fair and honest in our dealings with others, or change our passive attitude to life. Reaping as one sows is the law of karma.

"Do not be deceived: God cannot be mocked. A man reaps what he sows"
(Galatians 6:7)

*"Whoever has qualities is the doer of deeds that bring recompense;
and of such action surely he experiences the consequence."*
(Svetasvatara *Upanishad*, v, 7. – Hindu tradition)

Transpersonal psychology is a new approach in psychology that is interested in aspects of people that go beyond ordinary experience to matters of ultimate meaning, studying, for example, meditative and mystical experiences. Many books by writers in this field echo the idea of a mature stage of human growth when we start to take responsibility for our own development. Just a few or many may achieve this but, although individual transformation is necessary, it is an opportunity open to all. They say it involves pain and discomfort. This is because it means questioning all the roles one has been playing. Yet, there is more to us than just the rôles we play. We are not just a spouse, member of an occupational group, or sportsperson. If we identify solely with our rôle, we risk an identity crisis if we are compelled to lose it for example when our circumstances change and our rôle is no longer needed or viable.

Many therapists, who are concerned with their clients' well-being, try to help them to explore and work through any inner conflicts between different roles or feelings about which they were often not fully aware e.g. between being a parent and a worker, or between a fear of, and desire for, an intimate close relationship. In this way, the various parts of the personality can start to work in greater harmony together.

Psychologists often mention the notion of integration as a help to understanding personal growth. The various diverse desires, fears, ideas, hopes and aspirations become compatible with each other as the individual starts to resolve conflicts, choose priorities and find over-arching values. However to find this level of integration of the various sides to our makeup requires not just our hearts and minds but also bodily actions to be in harmony.

Taking the bull by the horns seems scary at first. After all it is easy to imagine the bull may turn round and gore us to death. But if we take courage we find that it is not so dangerous as we thought. We may have had no suspicion that there was any courage within us to be found. Yet my experience with many anxious clients shows that courage arose within when they started to take responsibility for their own development;

rather than passively allowing themselves to be swayed this way and that by the events of their lives; rather than complacently drifting through life. Having the deeply human faculties of reason and freedom, we can all take the initiative in creating our own world; not the world that society has tried to pre-ordain for us but rather the unique world of experience that we want for ourselves. That way we each find our true self.

"Everyone has what is truly human from rationality, in that he can see and know, if he will, what is true and what is good, and also that he can from liberty will, think, speak and do it."

(Swedenborg. *Divine Providence* section 227 [5])

4. Valuing Sex

Many of us are inclined to rebel when someone tells us what to do. We do not always take kindly to being told what is right and wrong behaviour. However, the world's spiritual traditions say that ethical living is part of personal development. That following a set of rules of conduct is conducive to spiritual growth. How does this apply to sexual relationships?

Infidelity

People may not be concerned about the rights and wrongs of sexual behaviour. They ask:

- "Isn't sex a basic drive that needs to be satisfied, just like hunger and thirst?"
- "Isn't sexual expression one of our inherent freedoms?"
- "Isn't sexuality a way of expressing our unique individuality?"

To answer "yes" to these questions may be correct for some but it is to miss a spiritual principle, for it ignores the idea of a growing union of mature love between two people. There are many reasons for coldness developing between a couple but one of the most damaging tends to be the sense of hurt and distrust in one partner caused by the other becoming sexually drawn to another person.

In Britain these days, people tend to speak as if it were tolerable to have more than one sexual partner as long as you do not deceive anyone. Consequently, a few people have a so-called 'open' relationship. More common is an apparent social norm of 'serial monogamy'. In line with this view, one should finish a sexual relationship before taking up with someone else. However many people in a relationship seem to be vulnerable to sexual wandering. A casual attitude to sex can lead us to make light of any indiscretions.

A lot of things in life, particularly in the mass media, seem to have become sexualised these days – from small girls' clothes to cars and even chocolate. It has been suggested that a casual attitude to infidelity can develop as one starts to watch extra-marital passions on TV or at the cinema. It also grows if we linger on the pages of a magazine with sexually provocative advertising, if we fixedly gaze at the figure of an attractive man or woman in a way that arouses sexual feelings or if we engage in any sexual fantasy not involving our partner. I would suggest that people more at risk are those without an interest in any productive activity such as study or business. This can result in a wandering desire. With nothing else to absorb our interest, it is perhaps only natural that our thoughts might turn to sex! But:

> *"I tell you that anyone who looks at a woman lustfully has already committed adultery with her in his heart."*
> (Matthew 5:28)

> *"Right action is to abstain from sexual lust"*
> (*The Noble Eightfold Path* of Buddhism)

Noticing an attractive person other than one's lover is naturally likely to happen most of the time. I would argue one can appreciate good physical looks while at the same time respecting the person. However, there are increasing degrees of disloyalty - for example flirting, spending time with this other person, sharing intimate confidences, lingering kissing or embracing as part of social greetings and farewells, not to mention engaging in physical intimacies when alone together.

Mature Love

Young adults tend to fall in love. Sometimes this is falling in love with love – romanticising the other person, as the embodiment of all we consider to be ideal. Sometimes this is called the 'halo' effect when we notice just one aspect of the other person that particularly appeals such as their bravery or kind-heartedness and become enamoured with just that one aspect regardless of their other characteristics. Sometimes our infatuation is really all about physical attraction, or the perceived glamour, power or wealth of the other person.

We might possibly be trying to fill loneliness or an emotional vacuum with a love relationship. Some psychotherapists have written about this kind of immature love. They say this follows the principle "I love because I am loved." "I love you because I need you." On the other hand they say that mature love follows the principle "I am loved because I love," "I need you because I love you."

In addition to giving, mature love implies other basic elements such as concern for the life and growth of the other, responding to their needs, respect for their uniqueness, seeing them as they really are and helping them to grow and unfold in their own ways, for their own sake and not for serving oneself. Seeing one's partner accurately is possible only when one transcends one's self-concern and needs, seeing the other person in the other's own terms. One needs to listen and to enter and become familiar with the private world of the lover, to live in the other's life and sense his or her meanings and experiences.

I believe the union of mature love preserves our integrity and paradoxically our individuality. When in intimate love two beings become one in heart and mind, Swedenborg calls it a state of 'conjugial love'. [1] By this, he partly means a deeper level of love in which the couple have grown closely together in mutual trust and affection.

Sexually Loving Only One Other Person

We can compare an interest in having more than one sexual relationship with having a desire for intimacy with only one lover. We can distinguish between love of the opposite sex and intimate love of one person of the opposite sex – between, on the one hand, a roving desire with, on the other, an exclusive commitment. The latter is a chaste kind of attitude. Chastity is a somewhat antiquated term in today's world. However, it conveys a sense of purity, innocence, and decency with respect to sexual partnership. It also unfortunately has a connotation of not letting oneself have any fun, and of prudishness, but this is not what Swedenborg means by the word. A chaste attitude for him is not to be confused with sexual abstinence. Rather it is primarily concerned with what is going on in a person's heart and mind - with the purity and cleanness of a person's feelings and thoughts. A chaste attitude is a deep desire for a one-to-one relationship solely with one other person.

In other words, sexual desire is not an unchaste thing in itself. However relationships of a sexual nature with someone other than one's spouse involves a disregard of the trust and intimacy that has been shared in marriage that is extremely hurtful to the innocent partner. The idea of extra-marital relationships is sometimes softened to such terms as: 'fooling around', 'sleeping around', 'flings', 'affairs' and 'dalliances'; suggesting that infidelity can be guilt-free and harms no-one. If people are not looking for a conjugial relationship, then it is possible to understand how they might come to believe in the myth that extra-marital relationships are harmless.

Conjugial Love

The aim within conjugial love is a closer linking of minds and a profound linking of lives in intimate friendship and love - the essence of a harmonious long-lasting personal and valued sexual relationship. On the other hand using another person as a sex object demonstrates a complete lack of true caring. It is not showing love to someone as a person, but simply using their body as a source of excitement, physical pleasure and perhaps conquest. Why cause hurt to one's partner by carrying on with someone else? Loose sexual conduct is likely to tie in with self-justification and a lack of interest in the ideal of conjugial love.

According to Swedenborg the origin of conjugial love is spiritual. The conjugial state mirrors the state that Swedenborg terms, the 'heavenly marriage' within a person. This is a harmony between feeling and ideas when a desire for what is good matches a wise thought. These do not harmonise for example when we are feeling resentful towards a workmate whilst realising we are being unfair. Another example is blaming a neighbour for a problem in the garden when one knows this to be unjustified. The spiritual state of the heavenly marriage can be present within even a single person who has no close relationships. Such a person would be ready to receive the spirit of conjugial love if a suitable partner became available.

Gender

Much controversy surrounds the subject of male and female gender roles. I believe neither sex is superior to the other – just different. Modern feminism is less concerned these days about proving women can do what men can do. Instead, it places more emphasis on feminine values and interests. We do well what we are interested in. This might be successfully helping to create a collaborative mood within a professional meeting or calm atmosphere within the home. Women tend to give importance to feelings and relationship whereas men tend to act in terms of rules, and what they judge to be right.

Thus the sexes complement each other according to their tendency to have different interests or, as Swedenborg would say, what they each love.

An objective stance is thinking about the external aspect of things whereas a subjective one is seeing things from a personal angle. Men have no exclusive hold over objectivity in their thinking but they tend to be more interested in this stance than women. Neither have women any exclusive orientation towards subjectivity but they have a tendency to be drawn to this approach more than men. In common parlance we speak of feminine intuition.

Partnership

In my view these differences are the basic reason why an erotic interest usually develops between the sexes; why male and female get together. They say opposites attract. When a man and woman are in harmony as to what they think and feel, do and say, then a conjugal partnership can potentially be formed. Each partner can develop to be a different side of the same coin; growing together they may become as one. The husband tends to love having ideas, ideals and projects to accomplish, whilst his wife tends to love nurturing and embodying them in their relationships together and with others.

Each individual sees their happiness in the life of their partnership. When the couple are devoted to each other and growing together spiritually, they increasingly act together as one unit – they are working in harmony. Seeing their ideas and feelings reflected in each other they are then drawn away from self-orientation. As far as their ideas and feelings are good, they receive heavenly innocence, peace, and tranquillity.

"Conjugial love is directed to and shared with one person of the other sex. Love directed to and shared with several persons is natural love, for man has this in common with animals and birds, which are natural creatures. But conjugial love is spiritual, special and proper to human beings, because human beings were created, and are therefore born, to become spiritual".
(Swedenborg. *Conjugial Love* section 48)

5. Working on Love

Introduction

Is marriage an impossible dream? Is it unrealistic to expect two people to live together happily for the rest of their life? These days in England for example, couples, more often than not, live together for some time before even considering the possibility of marriage; a very different way of looking at things from, say, the middle of the twentieth century.

What lies behind this change? Some would point to the availability of contraceptives that allow us to have a full sexual relationship for the time being without the long-term commitment of parenthood. Others would point to a less hypocritical society. We all know that nearly half of marriages these days end in divorce. It is asked, "Why pretend everything is perfect by getting married when it clearly isn't likely to stay that way in many cases?"

Another suggested reason for living together without getting married is to do with a fear of failure of the relationship in the full glare of public knowledge. At least in Britain this pessimism is perhaps not surprising given the high rate of marriage failure. People see cohabiting as having the advantage of being a private arrangement between two people not involving any socially recognised level of commitment and which can be finished as well as started relatively quietly.

Others would suggest cohabitation reflects short-term mutual convenience rather than looking towards a relationship characterised by commitment through thick and thin over a long period. Why get married, they ask, unless you are religious and wish the relationship to be eternally blessed and guided by God?

Where there is a lack of deep affection between married partners then they can begin to feel marriage as an onerous bond imposed by law and social convention that takes away any sense of freedom. An extreme example of this state of mind often arises from a forced arranged marriage. However, when there is 'conjugial love' in the marriage, the partners do not feel this way at all but feel happy and content about the ties into which they have entered. Happy marriages can last. Half of couples who marry do last the course, so rather a lot of people must be doing something right somewhere along the line.

Inward Affection

The topic of conjugial love was introduced previously. I see it as a gift from heaven that inspires each member of a couple to feel an ever deepening affection for each other. The religious view is that we cannot expect to sustain all the trials and tribulations of living together by our own efforts without help from the divine source of love. Whether we can fully receive this gift of love depends on our inner spiritual state of heart and mind. As mentioned in the previous chapter, I would suggest there needs first to be a receptive conjugial state of heart and mind within the person – the marriage of what is good and what is wise in us. For when we act according to what is wise in line with our higher principles, then implanted into us are good feelings that echo such ideas. Our feelings, thoughts and actions are in harmony. If we try to follow our conscience for example by doing our best for our family, being a good neighbour, or engaging in honest and fair dealing in everyday life, then, as previously said, Swedenborg's insight is that there is a linking between us and heaven that he called a 'heavenly marriage.'

This inner condition of our heart and mind enables us to experience feelings of affection when we get to know a compatible partner. Good feelings in one partner are complemented in corresponding right ideas in the other, the couple are thus drawn together and the two minds are more closely linked. It is this close linking of the two individuals in love that enables them to work together on the various problems that any partnership is obliged to face.

Doing Better

If we mainly base our relationship on physical attraction or infatuation, then we build it on sand. The trouble is the stability of our partnership may be unreliable if we draw together mainly for sexual reasons. Erotic can mean erratic. However, if also based on a deep level of affection, we build our whole relationship on solid rock. Nevertheless, even the best marriage will have its ups and downs and if the downs are not addressed coldness can set in. [1] One common idea is that none of us is perfect and we therefore need to continue to change something in ourselves if we are to survive the challenge of living with someone. What could we each do better? What new attitude could we adopt?

Resentment

There are many reasons for disharmony creeping into a relationship. I can describe a few of these. One is resentment. We can perhaps see where a male chauvinist attitude came from when men were obliged to work most of their waking hours to earn any sort of livelihood for their families. "It's the man's job to go out to work and the woman's job to do everything else." However, these days life is very different.

An unfair sharing of responsibility between partners can also arise from slowly changing circumstances that are not properly discussed. One reason for marriage breakdown can be inflexibility by one partner regarding who does what in the home, or if one likes to get their own way and the other is 'too nice' for their own good. There is so much to do and there are few rules these days as to who should do what – looking after the children's needs, housework, seeing to the car, maintaining the garden, organising the social calendar, earning the income, shopping, cooking, doing the decorating and house repairs, to name only a few. When only one person in the relationship is making decisions about finance, rules of children's conduct, or family holidays etc. then there is additional scope for resentment. A one-sided relationship in the end may not work if resentment ever surfaces and the submissive partner starts to assert his or her needs and point of view.

Insensitive Communication

Insensitive communication can cause problems. Some of us are born with 'thin skins' and others acquire them through life experiences that leave us feeling hurt. The result is the same – we read a little too much into what our partners say or do not say to us. Most of us are a mix of good and bad and our partner is quite capable of being insensitive by expressing irritation, a patronising attitude, intolerance, or whatever whilst actually saying something honest or constructive. If we happen to be a little touchy, we are at risk of noticing only the negative element of what our spouse is trying to communicate and ignoring the positive. Once stung we may quickly feel hurt and humiliated. We then sometimes over-react and there is a danger of a mounting level of tension as a tetchy conversation merges into a disagreement and then even a fully blown row.

The opposite problem to being thin-skinned is to be thick-skinned.

An example of this is when we ignore or do not take seriously our partner's critical comments. The result is our partner feels we lack care for them and it is tiresome for them to feel they have to keep repeating the message for it to stand any chance of getting through. And it is also tiresome for the thick-skinned person to be nagged!

Healing Rifts

Psychologists have studied long-lasting and happy marriages.[2] They have discovered that in such cases couples spend time together, and confide in each other and treasure their joint memories. Values and goals are discussed and decisions are made fairly, agreement sought and disagreements negotiated.

Getting a job done at work without too many hitches means not letting up on one's concentration, not giving in too easily when difficulties crop up and making a continual effort. The same is true of a sexual relationship. To prevent it falling apart it needs working on. What is growing needs nourishing. What is becoming routine and boring needs a stimulating tonic. What is damaged needs care and attention.

One member of the couple may take the initiative in trying to put right what has gone wrong. However, unless the other joins in then nothing is likely to happen. After all, it takes two to tango! One partner may stop excessive drinking or gambling but the other needs to let bygones be bygones and stop harping on about the past. She may give up an excessive time allocation for individual interests but he needs to help find alternative interesting activities that they can both share. He may learn to be more tactful when disagreeing about something but she needs to show appreciation and respond in kind.

When there is real love present in the relationship then the couple will each want to make the effort to work on their difficulties. They will each be prepared to make sacrifices, at times putting the loved one first, being honest and open together about their inner ideas and feelings, spending time together – in a word prioritising their relationship so that together they can face the challenges of life in a state of mutual love and support.

Sometimes a relationship gets so bad that at least one of the partners is sure that the marriage has reached a point of no return. A case of irretrievable breakdown might be the case, for example, where a partner continues to indulge an addiction, be abusive or unfaithful despite previous repeated promises to the contrary. However, before things get to this stage, if any behaviour out of keeping with 'conjugial love' is challenged, understood and acknowledged, there can be a chance of nipping any mistakes in the bud or even if necessary embarking on a full scale job of saving the marriage. This means a full-hearted commitment to the relationship – a difficult thing to achieve where there is pessimism in society regarding the outcome of any marriage. Yet, unless we commit ourselves to our partnership, how could we get through the rough patches that any living together relationship must face?

We can regard marriage as a deep, almost sacred, commitment. One person said:

"To love, you must feel emotionally safe - totally accepted, respected, and supported. Therefore, we don't criticise or strike out in anger, instead we gently request a change."

Loving partners can help each other develop as people. For example, she can soften his male egoistic conceit and he can moderate the female tendency to view things emotionally.

Any marriage is likely to become less satisfying as the novelty wears off and the need for security in young adult life reduces. Yet those of us who believe in conjugial love will have a confidence that this spiritual force will bring closer harmony and mutual trust and care to any relationship where the partners are really prepared to work together on their problems and difficulties.

"It is masculine to perceive from the understanding, and feminine to perceive from love"
(Swedenborg. *Conjugial Love* section 168)

When the understanding of truth which is with the man makes one with the affection of good which is with the woman, there is a conjunction of the two minds into one. This conjunction is the spiritual marriage from which conjugial love descends.
(Swedenborg *Apocalypse Explained* section 983 3)

6. Being Acceptable

Who does not want to feel acceptable among those people we see and know? Yet how many of us are very troubled in this area and fail to be our true selves as a result.

Are We Lonely?

Appreciating one's solitude – for example in the back of beyond – at times can be a source of refreshment and energy. Yet, sometimes being on your own does feel very lonely. Even when in a crowd or a group situation we can also feel lonely. Then our loneliness can come from feeling different from, and not belonging to the network of people with whom we associate at work, home and play. Friendship flourishes with having something in common and thus having shared conversation and activity – experiences that give delight.

Harry said he had a habit of making a daily entry in his private diary. One day he wrote that he was feeling alone with the weight of the world on his shoulders and no one caring about this. He hates feeling that no-one loves him or even cares what happens to him. He hates being alone. On the other hand, he tells himself that he has nobody to whom he can talk who would understand exactly how he feels. He believes that even the few people he calls 'friends' would not be able to relate to how he feels and so he would never share these feelings with them. He lives in shared accommodation which means he has to deal with people who he says 'fuss at him' or ask him to do this or that for them. He thinks that a solitary life is probably the best thing for him because when with people he has a 'bad attitude' towards them feeling such negative emotions as scorn, irritation, and impatience.

The Loner

If we are not at ease with ourselves, we will be ill at ease with people we meet. We may build a wall around ourselves and not allow others to look inside it. We may doubt there is anything of value we can share with them like a sense of humour, sparkling conversation, interesting ideas, or some useful knowledge. This is a fear that others will discover what we imagine to be our limitations. So we may find ourselves thinking, "I'd rather do it myself," "I prefer to be alone." Because we do not mix with others, people do not get to know us and we will lack friends and close relationships. Then we will feel even lonelier.

Yet, when something goes wrong in our personal world, we can get desperate for someone to talk to or a shoulder to cry on. We need to feed our natural hunger for human contact and relationship.

The True Self

Existential writers often suggested that if we related to others in a genuine way we would be less likely to feel lonely.[1] Authenticity is being oneself with others. The people we meet will see our true self and not just the persona; not just the act we put on for the sake of how others may see us. The sort of person, who believes that to be happy one must be approved of by most people one knows, is in for a hard time. He or she will continually be working to gain their good opinion. What a life of pretence to meet others' expectations. What a life of effort to keep up the act. Yet of course it is not necessary for an adult human being to be thought well of by every person met.

It is possible for us to reveal more of our genuine feelings and thoughts. When I disclose something of myself then others are also more likely to do the same. Only when this happens will the people we meet actually listen to and understand us, and include us in what is going on. We can really find human companionship when we come together with people with the challenge of give and take.

However instead we may communicate only in a superficial way without being open about how we feel. Then we are hiding behind a social or intellectual façade and as a result not getting close to anyone.

"The overtones are lost, and what is left are conversations which in their poverty, cannot hide the lack of real contact. We glide past each other. But why? Why? We reach out toward the other. In vain - because we have never dared to give ourselves"
(Dag Hammarskjold Secretary-General of the United Nations 1953-1961)

Close relationships amongst people involve empathy and a shared understanding. One cannot be lonely having an honest relationship with a long-lasting friend or intimate partner where there is mutual concern. Being part of a good relationship means opening up to the other person the things of the heart and mind.

Recognising our Humanity

Through talking with others we can find out what concerns other people and what values we share with them. It might for example be a shared unease about the environment of the local neighbourhood, the needs of some disadvantaged group, or something troubling the family. Then we can begin to find some shared meaning that will help us connect purposefully with others. There is thus one good thing about feeling lonely. It is the chance to be reminded, "I really care about people, and I want to be with them. I need to find out what kind of connection I need with somebody right now" And then we are encouraged to take an action immediately to reach out to somebody and make this happen.

Accepting our Imperfections

We may avoid disclosing our true self to others if we feel we are unacceptable to them. This can happen when a person privately makes too much of his or her failings and not enough of inner strengths. Noticing only our negative side, we forget that we are all a mixture of strengths and weaknesses. Actually, it is easier to acknowledge our good points if we can be honest with ourselves about our bad ones. It is easier for others to talk to us when they can see what is negative about us as well as what might be positive; after all no one is expected to be perfect.

If we keep quiet about our ethical values, our sense of beauty, or the uplifting ideas that inspire us, we will not reveal these feelings and thoughts either to ourselves or to others. No wonder loneliness and self-doubt may come about when we do not appreciate the better side of our nature and the deeper part of our own character. Only when we realise the reality of the spiritual qualities within us can we start to feel more at ease with ourselves, to hold our head up high despite our failings, to be authentic in revealing our true self, and to feel comfortable about others seeing us as we really are – 'warts and all.'

Need for Others

The prisoner in solitary confinement is separated from other prisoners as well as from communication with people in society, and he suffers for it. His basic social needs are not being met for we are all interdependent members of a universal humanity needing each other to some degree at least.

"No man is an island, entire of itself...any man's death diminishes me, because I am involved in mankind; and therefore never send to know for whom the bell tolls; it tolls for thee."

(John Donne)

The rest of us are usually in the physical company of other people – at work, at home and at play and we are only too aware of what they say and do. This means of course that we have to find a way of getting on with all these people; bosses, work colleagues, relatives, neighbours and friends. The emphasis is on our genuine involvement with others. This is the idea that people are not isolated from one another, but that humanity is interconnected. We need other people who sense our potential to encourage us as well as challenge us with the raw difficulties involved in having to get on with others to survive.

There is some analogy between Carl Jung's concept of a 'collective unconscious'[2] and Swedenborg's doctrine of a 'spiritual world.'[3] Jung's concept is that of a storehouse of mankind's legacy of human instincts, creative ideas and spiritual possibilities about which we are not directly aware. This is said to be the source of images seen in shared mythical stories and individual dreams. He distinguished this notion of a 'collective unconscious' from what other psychodynamic psychologists have called a 'personal unconscious' – an idea more familiar to the modern reader that is seen as a sort of repository of repressed individual experiences that influence the way we behave. Jung thought that archetypal images are collectively promoted within the mind – formative ideas conveying mysterious and deeply impressive messages. By learning from such symbols, he said the individual could better discover how to link together the various disparate elements within the personality. In other words Jung assumed that much of our unconscious life is influenced by universal themes we have in common with the rest of humanity.

A century earlier Swedenborg had had a similar notion that we are each unconsciously influenced by many others whom we never see. His idea of a 'spiritual world' is that of an unconscious source of our creative ideas, our thoughts, notions, impressions – all coming to us through the spirits of former earthly people now alive in a hidden dimension that is as real as the material universe. Spiritualist mediums have described this spirit world as a hidden realm which can be consciously experienced by those who are born with psychic ability and who have trained to get in touch with what they term the subtle promptings within the mind.

Of course ordinarily most of us have little or no direct awareness of such a realm.

No one is an island of self-generated perception. We all need other people even when we are physically alone in order to give us an inspiration and broader perspective. I believe that actually without an inflow of thoughts and feelings from the spirits of others we could have no meaningful perception, understanding, or motivation.

Noticing a Mystical Presence

We may recall once having been in a beautiful setting, perhaps with a sunset. We were relaxed and simply taking in all the natural beauty. The mood was one of patience and a relaxed perception of what was there. Then we suddenly and unaccountably felt as though we were part of the immense living, creative life before us.

This is a type of experience that many can remember having at some time or other. How can we feel alone when we sense being part of this mysterious life force? Our authentic relationship with this divine source of life is also an important part of our personal well-being.

Something happens when we are on our own that can only happen when we are by our self. It is finding a sense of what is universal within our limited ideas; the sense of timelessness and the eternal now; being alive to a transcendent truth and life. It is wordless and we cannot easily communicate it. It is like a presence that is so close to our inner self that we cannot easily share the experience with anyone and so it is often unheard, ignored, lost, in the hubbub of daily life. The effort to make space for it is too great. We need a chance to listen to, focus on and inwardly digest those hidden, sparkling moments.

Remnants of Childhood

These experiences may chime with dimly felt recollections of childhood; when we felt a sense of trust and no sense of urgency or responsibility; when we were spontaneous in our play and capable of joyfulness. This supports the idea that these innocent states of childhood remain deep within us as we pass on into adult life. We may no longer experience them much as we strive to succeed in our adult world. Nevertheless, unconsciously what remains within prepares us for those special moments when we can once again experience contentment and peace.

When parents are gentle and patient tolerating their children's imperfections then they act as a medium for the implanting of such heavenly states. On the other hand if their attitude to their offspring is possessive rather than caring, demanding rather than giving, then children will see through any false demonstrativeness of affection into the selfish impatience that lies within. If basic love is unconditional so that parents impose rules in a loving way then the child will trust and love their parents. However, if parents only attend to the child when he or she happens to meet their demands then the child will not feel trust and contentment.

Psychoanalyst John Bowlby has written about attachment and loss in maternal care and the development of the child. He wrote that an essential condition for the well-being and psychologically healthy development of the child is 'a warm, intimate and continuous relationship with his mother in which both find satisfaction and enjoyment'. Physical touch, as an expression of love, is vital for infants and, when not provided, its absence can cause severe emotional problems or even death. It is important that we as children felt the parent loved us for ourselves. In this way, I believe, we are ready to accept ourselves and accept the reality of a heavenly state within our soul and the love of a divine spirit. Parents are in the place of God in infancy. We can sense God's loving presence because we retain within us that sense of comfort and security we experienced long ago with our parents.

We may notice a mystical presence in the beauty of nature, in the love of a parent, but also in times of personal crisis. There was a man in his mid-twenties who reported being in a state of 'dire perplexity'. When the trouble first appeared he was dazed, but before long – about two or three hours - he could distinctly hear these words spoken inside of him, 'My grace is sufficient for you'. Every time his thoughts turned to the trouble, he could hear this quotation. He felt that God has frequently stepped into his life very perceptibly.

The Nature of God

However, what is God like? Cold or warm? Condemning or forgiving? Critical or accepting?

The abstract notion of the divine being is just that – an abstraction. The divine spirit is a perfect ideal that I cannot really conceive; being finite, how can I know the infinite?

"Measure not with words the Immeasurable;
nor sink the string of thought into the Fathomless"
(The Buddha. *The Light of Asia*, viii.)

This impossibility of conceiving the absolute is expressed by Jesus as:

"No one has ever seen God"
(John 1:18)

Yet, I think of the divine spirit as humane – the perfect human model of which we are all imperfect images – a Lord God with a heart of compassion, a wise head and powerful hands. The historical person of Jesus Christ revealed this divine human spirit. The Gospels tell us a lot about Jesus Christ himself. One who has a natural empathy with others and so with whom we can each relate, person to person.

It is difficult speaking to a stranger so it might help us to go over in our minds what we know about Christ – particularly the good things we have heard. He was not like the person who believes one must be approved of by everyone. He did not live a lie pretending to meet others' expectations. Instead he associated with certain individuals such as despised tax collectors and social outcasts knowing full well this would meet with disapproval. Just because not everybody approved of his behaviour and what he taught did not mean his disciples and friends did not accept him.

Those of us who assume we need to be approved of by all significant people also tend to think that other people should agree with what we ourselves think and believe. So we become anxious if we cannot persuade them to fall in with how we think about things. But typically, Jesus would say what he thought, and left it to his listeners to make up their own minds – even if this meant their rejecting his views and ultimately rejecting him himself. Jesus predicted his betrayal by Judas and denial by Peter. However, he did not alter his actions to gain their approval, nor did he beg for their approval. He simply continued on his course.

Many religious people would acknowledge that when they talk to him as their God then they often get answers to matters which perplex them. Not necessarily an inner voice but intuitions begin to dawn. Similarly Swedenborg's concept of the spirit of Jesus Christ is the divine presence within our own hearts and minds. [4]

On the one hand many parts of the Bible actually seem to say a lot of bad things about God; that he gets angry, wanting revenge, is hateful, and wanting to punish. On the other hand, I would argue strongly that these are only appearances of what is real about God's true nature, suited and adapted to the limited understanding of the relatively primitive mind. God is like a parent who, out of love and care, puts on an angry demeanour when their child puts its hand near an electric wall socket. Children do not understand adult ethics, nor does teenage idealism, but they can appreciate a moralistic tone. The mature adult mind however can see through the appearance and realise that actually a God of pure love can never really get angry let alone want revenge, be hateful or desire to inflict punishment.

The Gospels portray Jesus Christ as the divine humanity of God; loving, merciful and wanting to help us all. He healed the sick, went out of his way to teach those who wished to learn, and was a good friend to his followers. It is easier to bring to mind someone when we think of his character. Likewise, we can grasp God being with us when we remember all that he does for us, his children. A woman once said that she had the sense of a presence, strong, and at the same time soothing, which hovered over her. Sometimes it seemed to enwrap her with sustaining arms. This sense of inner support and friendship can come from talking, person to person, with Christ. Thoughts that are different from those that have been afflicting us suddenly come to mind after we start to do this.

I believe we can never feel lonely when we learn to get in touch with the humanity of God as the hidden uplifting force within our soul. We can especially hope to have contact with Jesus when we humbly ask for his presence. It is the divine within our being that comforts us, as when we are experiencing, for example, the anguish of loneliness, and that inspires us to express our true individuality in the way we relate to others. This is the loving acceptance we need if we are to set to one side the self-consciousness that formerly hindered our human contact.

"I will not leave you as orphans; I will come to you. Before long, the world will not see me anymore, but you will see me. Because I live, you also will live."
(John 14:18-19)

"It is the Lord's presence with man through angels and spirits, by and according to which the man is enlightened and taught".
(Swedenborg. *Doctrine of the Lord* section 46)

7. Gaining Self-Control

Our Immoderate Habits

Many of us have developed ways of acting that can annoy others or damage relationships. Examples include thoughtless untidiness, nagging, telling lies, and over-use of alcohol. The trouble is we have got used to letting our appetites and feelings get the better of us. Better to go about things in a balanced way.

"Temperance...which consists in not being transported by the passions, but in controlling them with coolness and moderation."
(Plato. *Phaedo* 68- Ancient Greek philosophy).

"Devotion to the pleasures of sense – devotion to self-mortification; by avoiding these two extremes he who has won the Truth has gained knowledge of that Middle path which gives vision."
(The Buddha. *Samyutta-Nikaya*, v, 421)

If we keep behaving immoderately, our habits become ingrained and we may think they seem impossible to change. Adults sometimes see the early clues to later maladaptive patterns of behaviour in the negative ways some children behave.

As children, we took on board certain positive and negative tendencies from parents, family and playmates. Later we developed them into either good qualities that help us function in the world, or self-defeating traits that do not – what might be thought of as our virtues and vices. Yet, we do not necessarily fix such traits in ourselves and what is learned can be unlearned. Just because we were 'a right little horror' when a toddler, it does not mean we will always be objectionable when older. As we become adults, we can gain better control over our behaviour but this requires a conscious effort and persistence. Otherwise, we are likely to continue to feel inner conflict, have incongruent ideas about things and experience difficulties of maladjustment.

Sometimes, even without realising it, one behaves as if one cannot help oneself. We say: "It does not matter what I try to do I am a victim of my past." "A leopard cannot change its spots." "Once a bad boy always a bad boy." This is the basic concept that whatever has happened in the past continues to be an all-important determiner of our current and future actions. Those of us who were brought up with a knowledge of the Bible are familiar with Jesus' attitude to this. He told a leader of a prominent religious party of his day that he must be 'born anew'. Our life does not have to stay the same. There can be a new start involving new ways of behaving and new attitudes. It is not true that we cannot change.

Often our family and friends are more aware of any problem behaviour in us than we ourselves are aware. We may not always realise when, and to what extent, we are at fault. It might help to find out from somebody else at what times and in what situations we are going wrong. It might be overspending money, over-eating, or being untidy around the house. To stand any chance of gaining self-control we need to be completely clear about why we want to change. What harm am I doing? What is embarrassing, upsetting or irritating for me or for others?

Our Free Choice

When we have got ourselves into a corner, dug ourselves into a hole, then we are obliged to re-think what we are doing. When the heart and the head are in harmony then the hands have the opportunity to start acting differently. We are all subject to negative influences but after all is said and done, there is nothing compelling us to be untidy or drink too much alcohol. It just seems that way at the time. Having a sense of freedom in choosing between alternative actions is a familiar experience. It confirms our ability to make real choices.

Many images from the mass media bombard us each day; the fastest and sleekest car, the holiday resort with the most sensual allure, the latest fashionable clothes. None of these things is bad in itself. However, each can feed our natural attraction to glamour, social status, bodily pampering; ego-oriented or self-indulgent desires which might rule our hearts. Having some connection with them does not mean we need enslave ourselves to them. Because these desires are not entirely part of us, we can distance ourselves from them if we choose.

However, without a conscious change of direction our hands will carry out their old habits. They seem to have an impetus of their own. If we fail to think about what we do we will continued to act like slaves to them. The first step is to use our heads. The head can understand the pros and cons of following the new or old ways. Secondly, a change of heart is needed, a new desire. It is never too late to stop a bad habit.

Nevertheless, a new resolve is not enough. How many New Year resolutions are broken within the first month? The third step involves the hands. This is acting differently as we actively struggle with our natural inclinations. It is the way we behave when we are most at risk of relapsing into our old ways and when we have reached that real choice between yielding to, or defying our impulses.

Spiritual Temptation

For many of us our spiritual values call us to a deeper conflict. This kind of conflict is not between pandering to our base desires and exercising self-restraint only for the sake of our own benefit. Instead, it is about what is dimly sensed as the prick of conscience. In other words, we are spiritually tempted when we experience an impulse to go against a principle of conscience that deep down in our hearts we accept as the spirit of truth operating in our lives.

I believe that we human beings are in a state of equilibrium between higher and lower influences, which sway us in opposite directions. In other words, we are in freedom to resist or yield to urges that originate from beyond ourselves. Like a battle within the person, temptation combat becomes inevitable. This happens when we try to control what is bad in our lives because it goes against our inner awareness of what is good and true. Usually we are only too well aware of this inner conflict.

> *"Difficult to conquer is oneself. But when that is conquered everything is conquered."*
> (*Uttaradhyayana-Sutra*, ix, 36 - Jainism)

Swedenborg himself experienced temptation combat. When in his fifties he had begun to reflect on his dreams and discovered a high level of self-regard in his attitude towards himself. He had always wanted to make a name for himself through his books but this form of self-love amounted to what he came to see as an arrogant and invalid thought that he could save himself from whatever was bad in his life by his own efforts and abilities. It contradicted a basic religious insight that there can be no redemption from our 'inner foes' without the aid of divine saving power.

Traditional Christian theology tends to emphasise a reliance on belief exclusively in God for salvation from our failings. There is an emphasis on the belief of the head, but in effect, this is at the expense of de-emphasising the heart and hands – thus diminishing personal responsibility for us to gain control over our own behaviour. Non-religious people understandably find this approach difficult to swallow. They also resist any inference that we humans have a bad side that needs purification and that we have no inherent goodness. It is as if they assume that, were this to be the case, it could only result in our apathy and despair: for it would mean a pessimistic view of human nature – that we cannot grow and heal ourselves by our own intelligence, effort and character – something they cannot accept.

I would say that neither the orthodox theologians of the eighteenth century nor the humanists of our own times are wholly wrong. Both seem to have a point. But is it not the case on the one hand, that morality is active and fruitful employment of one's powers? And on the other hand, are we not hindered in the quality of what we can achieve unless we open ourselves to and draw on divine inspiration?

Doing – coupled with the quality of our wanting and thinking - is what counts towards our character formation and destiny.

> *"Now that you know these things, you will be blessed if you do them."*
> (John 13:17)

> *"It is not the knowing that is difficult, but the doing"*
> (*Shu King*, iv, 8 – Confucius tradition)

> *"How shall you be saved without good works?"*
> (*Nanak*, I, 351 – Sikh tradition)

If we keep on failing to overcome a temptation, we can choose to ask God to take it from us. This can happen as long as we continue sincerely to try to resist what our conscience is warning us about.

A Higher Power

This teaching is similar to that of Alcoholics Anonymous (AA). Like S H Hadley, the man who sat in the bar in New York, many alcoholics feel they have failed, despite doing all they can, to overcome the 'demon drink'. The twelve step programme encourages members of AA to surrender themselves to a higher power many call God – to a belief that only with the strength of this force for good beyond themselves can they stay sober. No matter what our problem, we can all experience a huge sense of confidence that the battle can be won when we believe that we are not fighting alone. Yet we all have a part to play. For example, in the case of the problem drinker, it would be no good believing in a higher power without actually drawing on that power, by resisting the temptation to buy alcohol over the counter or visit a drinking establishment.

Likewise we can make a distinction between, on the one hand, the notion of resisting bad impulses by our own efforts alone and, on the other hand, resisting them in God's strength 'as of ourselves'. In other words, we need both divine strength and our own co-operation to turn away from what is wrong in what we do, and instead embrace the wiser path.

The Importance of Effort

The reasons for being out of control of our lives are often emotional. We may overeat because we feel we need comfort. We may compulsively gamble because we feel bored and seek excitement. We may be sexually addicted because we love the pleasure that comes from new conquests. The bad news is that if we make no effort to resist our own demons, no attempt to stop pandering to our primitive instincts at the expense of our higher impulses, then we have taken a backward step away from gaining any control over our faults.

If we do not do what we understand to be good and wise, what is bad in us will acquire more power over what is good in us. It may be asked why is this so? Would it not be nice if we could just change our habitual patterns of behaviour simply by better understanding them; just having a clearer self-insight? Actually, the answer to this is to point out that to heal the understanding with its thoughts and insights is to heal a person only outwardly. What needs also to change is the inward aspect of the individual – what is felt, wanted and chosen. Therapy for the understanding alone would be like palliative healing – failing to touch the inner malignity. Others may help us to express our feelings and reflect on them but also we need to compel ourselves to follow a wiser way of living.

> *"You yourself must make an effort. The Buddhas can only show the way."*
> (*Dhammapada*, 276. – Buddhist tradition)

If we do try hard to take control over our negative patterns of behaviour – the desires to get our own way in all things, the cravings for receiving attention and admiration, or whatever, – *and* look to a higher power beyond ourselves, then the religious message is clear. The divine spirit can give us a new character with a greater sense of freedom, and we will no longer feel out of control of our lives. [1]

> *"Temptations ... serve to subdue the cravings of self-love and love of the world and to make a person humble. That is, they serve to fit him to receive the life of heaven from the Lord, that life being the new life such as one who has been regenerated possesses."*
> (Swedenborg. *Arcana Coelestia* section 8966)

8. Finding Forgiveness

Our Mistaken Conscience

Not all that is going on in our mind is the working of a true conscience. Some of us find ourselves at times on a guilt trip. Even if we have a sound mind, we may sometimes feel guilty over the smallest thing – without rhyme or reason painstakingly worrying about something we have done that really is unimportant. One example is children who, having been trained by their parents to follow certain rules, like never putting one's elbows on the table at meal times – feel guilty when they have grown into adulthood if they ever break this rule. Other examples of illogical guilt are saying 'sorry' a lot of the time and unfairly criticising ourselves; trying too hard to get friends to like us, feeling easily embarrassed when asking for favours or doing anything that might displease them.

Many hopelessly sick people feel constantly guilty. This may result from the suspicion that their sickness and fate are self-inflicted and their own fault. Alternatively, they may assume, more or less, the rôle of the utterly dependent child. Some consciously apologise for the trouble and fuss they are causing. (Our Western culture fosters a sense of guilt in most of us when illness places us in the dependent role). If we are dying, we may even feel as if we are forcing the living to face the necessity of their own deaths for which we suppose they will not be thankful.

Psychoanalysis is interested in throwing light on our unconscious emotional impulses, and the conflicts between these and the demands of the real world around us. Feeling frequently guilt-ridden comes about from our worldly concerns – like wanting to be well thought of and desiring popularity. [1] According to Sigmund Freud, neurotic guilt should be approached by working through the sense of badness and the unconscious wish for punishment. People tend, in varying amounts, to be troubled by all manner of false guilt feelings resulting from a distorted, perhaps puritanical, viewpoint of human reality – and I would say that in the uncovering of such false guilt feelings, the Freudian psychotherapists have done a good service to the general psychological health of modern people.

We can start to feel a little less uptight about our behaviour when we see the unreasonableness of some of these guilt-laden habits of thought and learn how to face up to them. For example realising that looking after oneself does not necessarily make us selfish. If we did not spend money on food and clothes for ourselves, we would not be able to do useful work. If we do not have any respect for ourselves, how can we hope to respect anyone else? If we do not look after ourselves how can we expect to look after anyone else? As I have earlier suggested, if we can better accept ourselves for what we are – warts and all – then we will depend less on being looked upon well by those who know us.

If we can learn to notice our strengths as well as our failings, we will feel less bad about our mistakes. We can let go of some unpleasant guilt feelings and illusory ideas they tend to generate.

Our True Conscience

Our true conscience is more than mere knowledge in the head – it also involves the heart. It is different from unconscious fear of the ingrained experience of parental displeasure or disappointment in childhood that psychoanalysts point to in the notion of 'superego'. It is not the same as the feelings of shame triggered by social pressures about which some other psychologists talk.

Sometimes we act against a heartfelt and deep awareness of what we feel to be right – against a true conscience. We rightly feel bad about it even if sometimes we act in error on impulse without thinking.

> *"Anger, intoxication, obstinacy, bigotry, deceit, envy, grandiloquence, pride and conceit, intimacy with the unjust, this is what defiles one."*
> *(Sutta-Nipata, ii, 2,7. – Buddhist tradition)*

In other words, sooner or later, we all do foolish things. The existential psychotherapists have pointed out that one cannot reason away those guilt feelings which come from an awareness of actual transgressions against true conscience and unfulfilled potentials. The important thing is to try to disentangle feelings of guilt arising because of a true conscience from feelings of guilt arising from other causes. For example, it may be reasonable and fair to accept guilt about the avoidable bad things that we have done. No longer can the individual comfortably rely on such alibis as 'I didn't mean it', 'It was an accident', 'I couldn't help it', and 'I followed an irresistible impulse'. Such acknowledgment of guilt arising from a true conscience is helpful if it can lead to a change of behaviour. It is easier to feel a sense of being forgiven when we change our actions for the better.

Misguided Conscience

We may be being unduly hard on ourselves when we castigate ourselves for past wasted time, or unfinished tasks when we have been in a situation where we have been beset with difficult problems. It is easy to look back with hindsight and notice lost opportunities not seen at the time. The chronically sick person who blames him or herself for talents withering in disuse is listening to a mistaken conscience for no one can be expected to lead an active and full working life whilst struck down with illness beyond their control. How can one forgive oneself for such past behaviour when there is nothing one can do to make amends?

A couple had recently fallen in love and got married.[2] They were sublimely happy. But tragically within weeks of the wedding, the woman was given a diagnosis of cancer and soon found herself needing a mastectomy, radiotherapy and chemotherapy. She became bald due to hair loss, developed mouth sores and painful bowel movements and had to face the devastating likelihood of an early death with no chance of having a child. In order to be with his wife through her ordeal, her husband, who was a writer of world renown in his field, chose to stop writing and generally turned his life over to her fight against cancer. This was an emotionally draining responsibility. He assumed he could not voice his own needs because of her suffering. Not surprisingly she came to take his support for granted.

In the middle of this, he himself went down with a medium-term debilitating illness of unknown origin. Due to exhaustion he even stopped his daily meditation – a spiritual practice that had previously given him huge benefit. For over a year he completely submerged his own interests, his own work, his own life. Up to that period, writing had been his life-blood. He defined himself by his writing and when that suddenly stopped he was suspended in mid-air, so to speak. In other words, his mistaken conscience was dictating altruistic but psychologically unhealthy behaviour that could not last indefinitely.

He was to say that he would have done all this again unhesitatingly under the same circumstances but would have done it differently with more of a support system for himself in place. The grinding rôle of a full-time carer takes a devastating toll unless this is available.

The need for one to find a balance between one's own needs and the needs of one's family or one's work is quite a challenge these days with so many pressures to withstand - let alone the extra pressure of being a full-time carer. It is a mistaken conscience that gets us to perform our useful caring rôles without setting aside any time for ourselves – for our recreation and other personal needs.

Phoney Conscience

Although caring for oneself may be important, sometimes underneath our actions are mixed motives. We may do things ostensibly for others when our real motivation is also looking for what we gain in the situation for example the good regard of others or an escape from criticism. This is a phoney conscience at work. Cynics call this 'enlightened self-interest'. Spiritual teachers instead urge that we do not act wisely and well from the thought of reward and concern only for ourselves.

"Be careful not to do your 'acts of righteousness' before men,
to be seen by them."
(Matthew 6,1)

"Let right deeds be your motive, not the fruit which comes from them."
(Krishna. *Bhagavad-Gita*, ii, 47. – Hindu tradition)

There even comes a point when self-love amounts to vanity and narcissism. Are we worried about not shopping for the latest cosmetic? Perhaps a false conscience is at work. A true conscience would encourage us to care for ourselves – doing our own thing – as long as this does not totally ignore the needs of loved ones, or the values that give our life deeper meaning.

Blame Game

We may try hard to put the past behind us and forget what we feel ashamed of. However, the past keeps coming back to haunt us so that we may end up feeling miserable. This can happen especially when throughout our upbringing we have been repeatedly blamed for any sign of self-centredness and pleasure seeking. Freud has shown the damaging impact of those traditional religious doctrines that support an account of God in terms of a persecutory superego that looks down upon mortals, judging and often condemning their behaviour. Instead of finding a sense of self-acceptance that enables us to move on, putting the past behind us, we may instead feel we deserve condemnation or even punishment before this can happen.

Sometimes we may want to be punished in the hope that this will put things right. Perhaps we yearn for God's forgiveness but cannot experience this because we believe we deserve only his judgment. Many people hold – what I believe to be a mistaken view – that he is keeping a little book totting up our sins as well as our good actions so that we can be rewarded with paradise or be punished with hell-fire depending on which list is longer. They believe that they and others deserve to be blamed when they are bad. Instead, I believe our destiny depends – not on past behaviour but rather on our future character. Those who become considerate, compassionate and kind-hearted – no matter what terrible things they may have previously done – are destined to continue enjoying underlying heavenly peace and joy despite any circumstantial trials and problems. On the other hand those who never progress beyond a self-oriented self-serving attitude are destined to continue suffering underlying miserable states of mind despite any enjoyment of the pleasures of the moment.

Mistaken Attributions

We need to make a distinction between the experiencing of temptation and whether or not we succumb to it. After all, good and bad impulses and thoughts arise from what we see and hear on a daily basis from television and radio, from what those around us at work and home say in our hearing and from what we read in newspapers, books and magazines. They stir up associations in our memory. Without realising it, although inspiring or alluring images and ideas may stir us up, nevertheless we can take no responsibility for their rising up within us.

We should not take the credit for any originality they may inspire – only perhaps for the effort and work we put in to turning them into something worthwhile. Neither should we take the blame for any shameful desires they excite in us; unless we dwell on their fantasies, act them out and then justify to ourselves our indulgence in them.

> *"What goes into a man's mouth does not make him 'unclean,'*
> *but what comes out of his mouth, that is what makes him 'unclean.' "*
> (Matthew 15, 11)

In other words, it is not the having of bad ideas and impulses arise in us, but how we respond to them that begins to shape our character.

Swedenborg says that anything that is genuinely good comes from God and heaven and so we can claim no merit in ourselves for it. This is at the centre of the correct religious attitude. The trouble is this idea has been misused to justify the notion that we should focus on our religious belief rather than try to do good and useful work. Actually, although I believe God is the power of goodness itself and the source of all virtues such as patience, tolerance, and kindness, nevertheless we human beings should do our best to take on board these divinely inspired qualities. Leave us to our own ways of doing things, and we would not act well. However, divinely inspired goodness and light can shine through our actions. Turning in the right direction towards God, we act as a channel for heavenly influence on earth and we become suitable vessels to receive spiritual gifts that enrich our lives and help us gradually to grow in love and faith. What many Christians call being reborn. The religious person is saying that the motivation for all that he or she does that is good comes from heaven.

Some of us tend to feel guilty believing all the bad things we think come from ourselves. Yet, only extremely vain conceited individuals make a mistake in claiming credit for every good idea they happen to have. Surely if it is mistaken to attribute all virtuous impulses to oneself it is also an error to believe that we are responsible for all bad things we think? Can we really be blamed for all the shameful desires that pop into our hearts if we neither entertain them for long nor fall for their tempting allure?

For me the answer is simple. Is not the hidden influence of hell the source of all vice such as malice, cruelty or condemnation? All we can do is try to avoid hell's way. If we do not, then what is bad will stick fast to us and we will find it rather difficult to wash ourselves clean from all the dirt.

Personal Growth

Swedenborg taught that God is the source of pure compassion. Loving us as he does, he puts aside our faults and blemishes. Such a picture of the divine is one that accepts us fully regardless of any of our past flawed actions. Although God never condones our wrongdoing, it is an image of a forgiveness. For our experience of living is one of temptation to put self before other people and bodily pleasure before principles of what is right and good e.g. to act greedily, deceitfully, or unfairly.[3] God is just as much concerned for the cruel and evil-minded person as he is for the good person. In giving honest criticism to those in the gospel accounts who behaved badly, Jesus Christ encouraged them to change their ways and he revealed an inner attitude, not one of contempt, but rather of concern and forgiveness. For example in speaking to the woman caught in an act of adultery – a crime punishable by death in her culture – he explicitly said that he did not condemn her. (John 6:11). Likewise to the Samaritan woman he met at the well, who was living with a man not her husband (John 4:10), instead of criticism he offered living water.

He wants us all to be able freely to choose good over bad, sense over foolishness, rather than becoming or remaining enslaved to the powers of darkness. For this reason God entered into the material plane of life to overcome the forces of ill-will and malice by responding with love and forbearance. By his doing this, he preserved our inner freedom.

Ideally, we would always adopt good impulses and illuminating ideas. Nevertheless, there are many times, when we abuse these spiritual gifts, by indulging in the bad desires and illusory notions that keep impinging on our hearts and minds. In other words, it is we at times who often distance ourselves from the divine by acting out base urges and following mistaken or self-centred notions. One example is when we continue to hold a grievance or feel resentful towards someone who has wronged us rather than adopting a forgiving heart. How can we expect to experience the forgiveness of others or to be able to forgive ourselves - let alone the forgiveness of God for our own wrongdoing, if we do not develop a forgiving heart towards those who do us ill. It is we, and not God, who create our resulting unhappiness.

What is bad in our behaviour brings it own reward. If we drink too much alcohol, we suffer cirrhosis of the liver and may lose our livelihood. If we go round, being nasty to people we will soon not have any friends and will become a social outcast. Bad behaviour results in bad consequences. It is we who tend to guiltily condemn ourselves for any wrongdoing. A God of love and wisdom cannot condemn anyone but only continually try to help us in the predicaments we create for ourselves.

Only by responding to the still small voice of our inner conscience can we hope to resolve to change. Swedenborg concludes that what is needed is acknowledgement of error, heartfelt repentance and sincere resolve not to repeat the error. We can experience a guilt-free state of peace and contentment if we, like little children, innocently allow God to lead us in all we do instead of primarily following our own agenda and own misguided self-interests.

*"There is divine, that is, infinite love; and there is divine, that is, infinite mercy...
(that) continually excuses, and continually forgives."*

(Swedenborg. *Arcana Coelestia* section 8573 [2])

9. Calming Anger

Normality of Anger

Have you been hopping mad recently? Some people temperamentally seem to be more easily roused to anger than are others. Yet, to some extent we all get irritated at times. We feel cross when others attack what we love, like our child or pet animal for instance. It could be something we love in ourselves that, when attacked, causes us a sense of wounded pride. We may experience 'road rage' in our heart, reasoning defensively in our head about it being the other driver's entire fault. We might then use our hands to make rude gestures or write letters making unreasonable demands. Offensive putdowns thrown at us in a condescending tone of voice can also get to us. Then irritation easily spirals when we retaliate in kind and the heated things that are said – which on reflection we often do not even mean – hurt both parties. It is possible to harbour resentment for years, especially if we continually avoid someone or allow ourselves to slip into the habit of not conversing with them when we do have an opportunity.

Making Up

Making up may be easier said than done. In addition, not every attempt at reconciliation works. We need to eat a little humble pie even if the other person does not. The trouble is, as Harold Coffin said:

"The fellow who thinks he knows it all is especially annoying to those of us who do"

Even when we swallow a bit of pride the other person may not stop his or her ego trip. Unless the opponent meets us halfway, the attempt at finding a way forward may possibly fail.

To increase the chances of success we could try saying what we think in a low-key way. By seeking a common understanding, we are giving the relationship every chance to get past this difficulty. It means looking at the situation from the other person's point of view; not assuming that he or she is entirely at fault, using our imagination to step into their shoes whilst at the same time not avoiding thorny issues. It is possible to explain our feelings without exaggerating and without casting blame. We can try to think of there being different points of view rather than one wrong one and one right one.

Sometimes we do not try hard enough to make up and rarely are we the first to make a conciliatory move. One fallacy is to believe that "a relationship that needs working at is not worth having." However, satisfying relationships are unlikely to develop unless all concerned are prepared to be committed and to make an effort.

We may wrongly assume that the other person who has hurt our feelings should know how hurt and angry we feel. Yet people cannot see into each other's minds and however close we are to others, they will never be able to know exactly how we feel unless we let them know.

Good Sense

We need to show good sense when relating to others. Making unwise compromises that maintain destructive relationships is not good sense. In other words, doing good to others and forgetting their wrongdoing may not always be wise if the behaviour is harmful and persists.

Violence within the home and sexual infidelity are two more serious examples. Acceptance of the other person's limitations rather than simply saying we forgive them may be a more realistic goal if there is no remorse or effort to change. In extreme cases sometimes it is better to part company.

Letting go of very deep-seated hurt may take considerable time that requires real or imagined encounters with the perpetrators of our pain. A few of us have been so very badly abused and offended against that it has caused a long-lasting suppressed state of anger. We may firstly need professional help to work through our shock and denial and become more aware of the effects of the terrible wrong done to us. This may involve starting appropriately to express feelings to others of hurt, grief, anger and rage. It greatly helps if the fact of the wrong-doing is acknowledged by those previously involved.

Desmond Tutu was a black clergyman living in South Africa during the apartheid period [2]. He and many other black Africans had every reason to feel very angry at the treatment meted out to them by the white supremacists in power over them. Separate public facilities were enforced on racial lines. To all intents and purposes only white Africans had the vote. Black Africans were legally confined to rural reserves covering only about 7% of the country whereas they consisted of 68% of the population. Segregated townships for blacks working in urban areas were set up. Blacks had to carry a passbook identifying themselves and showing whether they were entitled to be in a white only area. Husbands and fathers were separated from their loved ones as a result of a pernicious system of migratory labour. Their children went to overcrowded schools in black townships and lived in inadequate shanty housing with a woefully inadequate system of transport. Black people who protested suffered long periods of detention without trial and there were deaths in detention. All this meant that the black people suffered frustration and humiliation. They were a subject people.

Although not a pacifist, Desmond strongly believed in responding to injustice by asserting one's human dignity and rights in a courageous way with a view to possible reconciliation rather than revenge. He advocated civil disobedience rather than violence as a response to oppression. But when he and others joined illegal protest marches they risked being shot by police. Desmond, with other religious leaders, often intervened to try to help diffuse situations where violence was a distinct possibility, calming down the anger and aggression. This was the action of someone who believed that problems could be solved by people sitting down together to discuss their differences rather than resorting to violence. He said that the campaign should be characterised by discipline and dignity because they were all involved in a moral struggle and that only non-violent protest could succeed, resulting in their freedom. There were outbreaks of violence by black people but the overwhelming response to the violence of oppression was peaceful protest. Despite the great anger felt, the struggle was to be based not on hatred but on the hope of freedom and reconciliation.

Many commentators had thought that bloodshed, violence and civil war were inevitable because a people can take only so much injustice and despair. But they were wrong. In my opinion international pressure and the emergence of political leaders of the calibre of Nelson Mandela and Frederik der Kerk were necessary for the avoidance of civil war but what was crucial in this outcome was the prevalent spirit of love and justice in the nation – other than within the white right wing reactionary forces. The spirit of love was the message of the New Testament when Jesus said 'Love your enemies' As has been said, if instead we were to follow the old idea of revenge embodied in the teaching of 'an eye for an eye' soon all people would be blind and then where would we be?

It may be useful in our personal lives for us to try to see justice done and restitution occur and even attempt to ensure that the offences will not happen again. Some of these developments may help us to start to be reconciled to the offender in our heart, to let go of our anger and to move on with our life. There is no chance of finding a forgiving attitude if we harbour resentment, revenge or hatred. Alternatively we create continuing problems for ourselves if we try to forgive someone before we adequately explore and resolve our own feelings.

Our Inner Attitude

As we experience normal life and have thoughts, emotions, memories it appears to us that we are living from ourselves; that we are thinking, feeling, and remembering from a life originating in ourselves. This view differs from Buddhist teachings that regard the individual self as a delusion, and teach that spiritual progress depends upon recognition of this fact. Another Eastern religion, Jainism, takes a similar view. [1] The Western world, however, prizes the self-made man; individuality being valued in and of itself. We each have a strong sense of being the source and originator of all that goes on inside of us.

Subjectively, this is how it seems to us. It appears as though we are living from ourselves; that all our creative ideas, imaginings, desires etc. originate in our own minds. Any clever thoughts, for example, are our own self-intelligence. Yet, this subjective sense of self-originating being, that Swedenborg calls 'proprium' [3] – a term whose root meaning is 'what belongs to oneself' – is actually an illusion. I would say that it is illusory because there is nothing really that we can claim credit for as our own. Just as I believe that all that is alive in the world comes from the creative source of life, so also all helpful thoughts, all original imagination, all good affections of the heart flow from this same creative divine spirit working within all our hearts and minds. All bad or negative feelings and thoughts are due to our unconsciously distorting and sometimes perverting what is flowing in from this divine source. It just seems to the individual that he or she is a self-sufficient person separate from this inspiration and that we each produce these thoughts and feelings ourselves.

The good thing about proprium is that it allows us to take responsibility for what we do and say. Unless we sense that whatever we think and feel is our own, we could not so readily accept that we are actually accountable for our choices in what we do with them.

However, because of this self-sense termed proprium we tend to see things from our own perspective, often in a state of self-consciousness. Each person will see what is going on, say at a shared family meal or any other situation involving others, in a slightly different way, according to individual pre-occupation. For example one person might notice whether a certain topic about which he or she has strong feelings crops up in conversation. Another person might be sensitive to what others imply regarding their own personality and a third may be concerned with who else is helping in the kitchen.

This is all very normal if it does not interfere too much with the way the person functions within the group. However there is a danger that we might drift into an attitude of regarding most things from our own point of view and our own desires. Our modern society does not always frown upon self-concern. There is even a philosophical doctrine called 'egoism' claiming that morality has its foundations in self-interest. However, if we were to allow a self-centred attitude to dominate our thinking, there is a good chance we would soon become, not only selfish, but also self-pitying, hard-done-by, or conceited and boastful.

We do tend to get angry when our own concerns are threatened. When we are self-preoccupied and do not heed the feelings and needs of others, our pride is more easily pricked, our desires threatened, our fears aroused, and thus our anger more easily provoked. Probably at some time or other, we have all become bad-tempered when we could not get our own way. Actually some of us behave as if we believed it is important to always have our own way.

Which one of us could have done what Christ did (without anger) when he discovered that his ministry in Judea had resulted in his rejection and ultimately his death penalty. Due to his selfless heart he accepted the situation rather than trying to impose his will.

It is true that he is said earlier to have overturned the tables of the money lenders in the temple. (Matthew 21:12). But is there not a difference between a zeal associated with a selfless heart and a hostile anger arising from self-interest? The way I see it is that Jesus was demonstrating a zeal (rather than anger) for what is right and proper.

Whether we can let go of angry feelings depends on our underlying attitude. If it is feeding off selfishness and the attitude of 'every man for himself' or 'put the other fellow down', then our anger will persist underneath the surface, and apparently making up with someone will not extinguish it. Rather, it would be quick to be re-kindled whenever we next felt slighted.

However, I believe that if our self-concern is not active, we will be able to let go of our anger more easily because it does not run deep. This approach to overcoming angry feelings is noticing and challenging any threatened or damaged self-concern in us. It also means adopting a tolerant attitude, looking for the good in the person who has angered us, and being ready to accept that we are all in need of forgiveness.

"Anger is the general emotion that results from anything which gets in the way of self-love and its desires"
(Swedenborg *Arcana Coelestia* section 357)

10. Valuing What We Do

Monotony and Boredom

The ideal of job satisfaction may seem a little idealistic to the average person. It is all very well to become lost in your work if it is an interesting profession, like teaching, the arts, or law etc but people can often assume that other jobs like house-keeping, gardening or labouring are necessarily uninteresting. To many people, work seems to be a humdrum monotonous time that goes on and on involving much the same thing day after day. Wondering how we can avoid boredom with endless time stretching out in an eternal future may well put some of us off the idea of immortality. For others, being a small cog in a big factory or organisation, it may be hard to see that we are contributing any real service to the community.

Positive and Negative Motivation

However, the attitude we bring to a job can have a big effect on whether or not we find it boring. Do we have negative or positive reasons for what we are doing at work?

Humanistic psychologists often suggest that when we lack something, then they are negative reasons that are tending to motivate us. Examples of this would be, wanting a job for extrinsic reasons for example for the sake of the wage because we are short of money, or wanting it for the sake of the experience and training that could help us towards a needed occupational qualification, or doing favours for our work-mates because we fear they might otherwise cold-shoulder us. These are understandable motives albeit negative ones.

On the other hand, positive reasons can motivate us. This would be when we do something for intrinsic reasons inherently to do with the activity itself. For example wanting to study science at college because this stimulates an increasing fascination with the world of nature, or wanting to work hard because we value getting a job done well and on time. Being mainly 'growth motivated' in these positive ways means that the individual will be less dependent, less beholden to others, less needful of others' praise and affection, less anxious for honours, prestige and rewards. He or she does not require continual satisfaction of their needs through interpersonal interaction and in fact may at times feel hampered by others and prefer periods of privacy. [1]

Other-Oriented or Self-Oriented

Interpersonal interactions at our place of work oblige us to take account of the needs of others and this is quite a challenge.

The negatively motivated individual relates to others, from the point of view of self i.e. from what they can provide for him or her. I suggested previously that anger as opposed to zeal derives from self-centredness. If people do not meet what we feel we need, and self-orientation were to dominate our character, then we might tend to overlook them. We might well regard such people as an irritant or a threat. Children get off to an unfortunate start in life if their parents pamper and spoil them. Then they have to unlearn the idea that happiness can only come from having one's own needs met first.

Likewise, if we have a neurotic striving for affection, this will influence our whole attitude to other people whom we will see mainly in our own egocentric terms. We will be primarily concerned about satisfying what we see to be an unmet need for reassurance. It is as if we were constantly saying: "You won't hurt me will you and so you do love and approve of me, don't you?"

We thus strongly want affection, attention or approval that can never be satisfied. We may well become stuck in these patterns of behaviour as adults if we have been tragically hurt and disapproved of as children.

On the other hand, when we are growth-motivated we do not relate to others as 'sources of supply' to meet some shortage or deficit or perceived unmet need in ourselves. Consequently, we are able to view others as complex, unique, whole beings in their own right. We become more aware of their problems, talents and interests and thus give ourselves a better chance of having something meaningful to talk about together. We cannot help someone if we have not noticed what he or she needs.

It is possible to respond to people in one of two ways – one of which is self-oriented and the other is not. On the one hand each of us could look to what is good for 'me' in the situation – in other words for the sake of self-interest. On the other hand, we could look for the good for all in the situation – that is for the sake of the spirit of usefulness. By thinking of the benefit of those we are doing things for, we learn to be less egocentric and more sensitive to the needs of others seeing things through their eyes. We cannot put others first and put self first.

Signs of self-preoccupation include a sense of grievance, frustration, or self-pity. Choosing to do something helpful for others is a good way to interrupt these feelings. Then we may become more contented and calmer individuals. Taking pleasure in being useful deters us from asking 'How can I have some pleasure?' We think instead of 'How can I be of use such that we can all be happy?'

Self-Indulgence

Sometimes when we have been working long hours or are due for a holiday, we yearn for a chance to be lazy, and we might even think we could live quite happily if we never saw an office desk, vacuum cleaner or tractor again. However, when we overdo the holiday we tend to get lethargic and self-indulgent. When we sit and do little for a long time, then we find we have little to talk or think about, other than what is to do with self; whether it be how to find physical pleasure, get some excitement, beat others in the fashion stakes or make ourselves more popular. If all the time people occupy themselves with entertainment, parties, food and other bodily pleasures then they miss out on the deeper satisfactions that come from involvement in useful activity. Self-indulgence can be harmful if it becomes a way of life. But we are less likely to feel tempted by such things when we are regularly involved in some positive rôle. We are more likely to be tempted when we have all the time in the world to fall for whatever our particular personal weakness might be.

Usefulness

Having a positive reason for doing something means looking for what is useful in the situation. Being useful keeps us physically fit as when we engage in housework, gardening, or 'do it yourself'. Getting on with something can keep us mentally fit too, e.g. study, report-writing, or problem-solving at work. A useful life trains individual maturity as we learn to take the rough with the smooth.

I would suggest that it is not the nature of work, so much as the way we do it, that can give satisfaction. It is the attitude of mind we bring to the activity that affects how the job appears to affect us. The more we put into the situation then the more we will get out of it. By sincerely, fairly and reliably performing whatever useful tasks for which we are responsible – whether that be as parent, housekeeper, farm labourer, shop assistant, or businessman, etc – believe it or not, we can experience a deeper sense of delight that goes beyond and lasts longer than any physical or bodily pleasure. In other words, the attitude we bring to our duties affects the quality of the way we relate to others. Every person we meet can walk away from us feeling just a little happier. This can be because of the way we deal with them, the effort we put in, and the interest we have shown. Other people will have learned to rely on us to do what is needed without being prompted. They will have come to expect us to put proper feeling and thought into what we do. Their appreciation can give us huge satisfaction.

Having a caring involvement with one's family and friends or carrying out paid employment or voluntary work for the community – all these activities can be a challenge to the heart and mind that makes every day alive with opportunity and interest. By not being idle and being effective in what we do, we have no time to get bored. Not that being busy should become an end in itself. We all need time out for rest and recuperation.

People who are involved in what is going on around them, doing something even in a small way, can feel that they are giving of themselves as unique individuals and find in that giving, a sense of contentment. Often they find a wonderful sense of pleasure in doing a job well. [2]

"Each (individual)...has his particular contribution to make; for any one use is composed of innumerable uses...all and each co-ordinated and subordinated in accordance with divine order, and taken together making and perfecting the general use, which is the general good."
(Swedenborg. *Heaven and Hell* section 392)

11. Facing Our Flaws

Self-Assessment

People suffering states of anger, anxiety or depression may ask a psychological therapist for help with this distress. The fact that counselling or therapy has been sought suggests that there is an awareness that, although these feelings may be related to troubled relationships or challenges in life, a negative side of the person needs to be addressed if he or she is to change the way with which these are dealt.

Schools of Psychotherapy

Different schools of therapy use different theoretical terms to look at this negative side. For example, in the writings of Sigmund Freud, the 'id' is said to be amoral, illogical, self-serving and ruled by desires that only give self-gratification – for example for sex, food, and aggression.

According to Carl Gustav Jung, we each have a shadowy aspect that we have no wish to have. It is said to be the sum of all the unpleasant qualities one wants to hide, the inferior, worthless and primitive side of our nature, one's own dark side.

Similarly, Harry Stack Sullivan has said one of the ways we see ourselves is the 'bad me'. This is said to represent those negative aspects of oneself that we do not like to acknowledge, even to ourselves, and which we hide from others. Any anxiety that we feel, is said often to be the result of recognition of this undesirable facet, such as when we recall an embarrassing moment, or experience guilt from a past action.

Transactional therapists – using the ideas of Eric Berne – encourage self-insight into the negative side of personality, by examining the ways the individual interacts with others in so-called psychological 'games' that are said to be played [1]. They look for signs of an unacknowledged destructive attitude that can lurk beneath the surface of social interactions only to emerge quite dramatically as a payoff at the end of a conversation. One well-known example is when an individual presents a problem to others in a social context, such as saying 'It never works' whenever he or she tries to mend a minor fault within the home. The others start to present solutions, each starting with the words 'Why don't you...' To each of these the person objects with a 'Yes, but...' rejecting each suggestion with some plausible reason until they all give up. This shows that the interaction should not be taken at face value. A crestfallen silence has been engineered which gives expression to the individual's idea of personal inadequacy, amounting to self-dislike, coupled with his or her belief in the worthlessness of other people, a notion which had been privately held all along.

Other attitudes that Berne has uncovered in analysing such 'games' are pleasure in boosting oneself at the expense of others and expressing hostility. Underlying such attitudes is a belief that others and/or ourselves are not okay – that there is something inherently bad about them and/or us. When we express such feelings, we prevent our relationships – say with work colleagues or family members – from thriving or we even do great damage.

I am reminded of a scene from the Bible where the mythical Noah drank too much wine, became drunk and ended up lying naked in his tent. Ham, one of his sons, noticed his father's shameful state but did nothing to protect his father and instead made a point of telling others about it. However, his other two sons took a garment and, walking backwards, so that they did not see their father's nakedness, covered him up. They did not focus on his fault nor mock him as if he were worthless.

Self-examination, that takes place during the course of talking therapy, can uncover such mind-sets. Which of Noah's sons do we each resemble? When we look for what is bad in others or in ourselves, then we seek to put them or ourselves down. It is so much more healthy to look for the good in others and in ourselves.

Honest Self-Evaluation

Therapists want to help us to understand the different sides of our character. This honest self-examination is central to the work of all therapy that focuses on self-defeating behaviour. The different terms used for the negative aspects of our life, some of which I have mentioned, are in effect individual flaws. I must admit I have yet to know anyone – including myself - who does not appear to have some sort of personal flaw – not that it is necessarily our fault. The therapist helps clients develop self-insight into their negative side by throwing light on assumptions and fears about which people are often not conscious.

Swedenborg would say that we have a rational mind, that transcends the fears of the moment, which we can use to appreciate better the inner truth about ourselves; also that we can look at our own behaviour in the light of the values to which we ascribe. In this sense, self-assessment is also self-evaluation.

In other words, we may need to wake up regarding the darker shadowy [2] aspect of our makeup. We can hope to tackle it only when it emerges into daylight. This part of ourselves is what we have strengthened whenever we have continued to entertain some unworthy fantasy, even if we have not been acting out such fantasies. Despite these harmful tendencies in many of us, I believe that there is a divine spirit of what is good and wise present within our soul, if we are willing to attend to it, which points out a better path for us to follow in life.

Ed, a young Asian British man, [3] was willing to attend to this spirit of wisdom. He showed his willingness honestly to examine his dark side in the light of his inner knowledge of rational ideas. At the age of sixteen, Ed, who had been brought up in a devout British Muslim family, had become an Islamic fundamentalist, much to the horror of his parents. He had joined those who played politics with Islam, knowing how to use religion to manipulate the emotions of its followers to sympathise with terrorism and the setting up of an imaginary Islamic state. The values of tolerance, respect and compromise had had no meaning for him. He had wanted to destroy the Western democratic world. He had joined with others to do their best to whip up fear amongst Muslims. They disrupted peaceful religious meetings, and verbally abused those who resisted them. He had been hooked into a desire for power and dominance.

However, as he grew older he began to examine what he had got himself into. He began to question his motives and was to become ruthlessly honest regarding the errors into which he had fallen. As a result, he recovered his faith and mind and broke away from the fanatics.

During his childhood, he had previously gained insight from his religious parents regarding the spiritual way. Knowing where this path goes means knowing when we are wandering off from it and falling down.

Losing our way is not conducive to our and others' well-being. I would say that examining the 'bad me', the 'shadowy side', the psychological 'games' we may play, that is to say, facing our flaws – our mistaken path – is a crucially important first step towards personal growth. By doing this we can gain insight into the misguided nature of the assumptions we have been making and the way we have been abusing our position.

Self-knowledge

None of us can escape from some of the normal difficulties associated with human relationships. Problems may arise when talking with tiresome in-laws, troublesome neighbours, or angry work mates. Sometimes we deal with these situations using our flawed negative side, perhaps showing for example impatience, intolerance or rigidity. After all, no one is perfect. When we get it badly wrong our nearest and dearest may soundly tick us off.

It is all too easy to try to deny any personal criticisms that come our way. No one finds it comfortable to acknowledge shortcomings in their makeup. However, when we do notice repeated feelings of resentment, guilt, suspicion, frustration, hurt or worry, we might wonder if these are signs of faults in the way we are dealing with others. We may not be drawn into international terrorism, but are we always willing, like Ed, to own up to our own failings? Do we make an effort to observe what we do or say that is unhelpful, unjust, or downright selfish? Do we have self-knowledge?

One of the central planks of inward thinking is the examination of oneself in order to gain knowledge about our individual foibles; those negative tendencies within our makeup that we keep falling for.

"The ungoverned has no knowledge of himself"
(Krishna. *Bhagavad-Gita*, ii, 66 Hindu tradition)

Being honest with oneself about one's shadowy side can lead to apt changes of direction. We may start to give up old habits and change what have become familiar and comfortable attitudes. Some of the illusions we have built up about ourselves may be shattered. Yet giving up an unworthy activity or self-defeating way of relating to someone – although difficult – can be possible as long as we can overcome the obstacles to change.

Vulnerability and Proprium

One of these obstacles arises from what Swedenborg terms 'proprium', that was mentioned in the chapter on anger. Proprium (a Latin term meaning what belongs to oneself), is our inborn sense of self-hood and independent self-identity. I would maintain that it is because we are immersed in the physical sensations coming from the world around us and our bodies, which are part of that world, that we create our own pessimistic ideas, downbeat feelings, and self-centred desires when we do not get all we want. We then allow such negativity to imprison us. We imagine that we are separate from the force for life that created us and that inspires all that is good. I think it is because we do *not* disown the various negative features that each school of therapy has correctly identified, that we are more vulnerable to being ruled by what is negative.

Hearing the Quiet Voice of Conscience

There may be times, like with Ed, when we no longer have in the forefront of our minds the clear wholesome principles that we grasped as children. For example, perhaps we have started ignoring someone, even though this means that important disagreements with that person never get a chance of being resolved. We may have neglected the principle of making an effort to live harmoniously with others. Alternatively, perhaps we have the habit of putting someone down or gossiping about them behind their back so that friction and disharmony grow rather than reduce. We have forgotten the value of looking for what is good in others.

Yet, I believe what stays in us is a hearing ear and an understanding heart. Even when we are off the right track we can still be dimly aware of our mistaken ways, albeit hearing the voice of conscience [4] at times in an indistinct sort of way; the quiet voice reminding us of our responsibility for getting on with people.

It is Never Too Late to Change

There is nothing wrong with enjoying life's pleasures, nothing wrong with showing off, or engaging in other forms of self-orientation if kept in proportion. We cannot help our family or friends if we do not also look after ourselves and meet our own basic needs. However, if we take concern for ourselves to extremes, wanting to get our own way in everything, we will be attempting to dominate everyone around by virtue of some imagined superiority. A hellish state of mind is one ruled by self-centredness and pride. Indeed, in its most fanatical form, this becomes the love of being adored and idolised. Psychologists have labelled this self-absorption as 'narcissism'. In addition, self-love out of proportion can even amount to despising everyone who crosses our path, resulting in our harbouring malice, contempt, revenge, or cruelty.

Sensual pleasure may be very good in its right place. However, it is the sensual plane of our mind where the fixations, the addictions, the compulsions, and the sexual disorders can arise. They develop when we want to take delights of the senses that bit further each time to get the buzz – the excitement that comes from further acquisition, or further sexual exploration. Then addiction to pleasure rules the heart, more and more is demanded. For example, the individual can become addicted to sexual pleasure with many and different kinds of partner with the trouble this causes, as covered previously in the chapter on infidelity. Alternatively, there can be a preoccupation with financial gain, working all hours to make that further profitable business deal, regardless of the personal and family costs involved. Money may be fought for tooth and claw because it can buy all kinds of worldly pleasure or be spent on things that symbolise one's worldly status.

> *"Pondering on objects of the senses there springs attraction; from attraction grows desire; from desire is produced passion; from passion comes delusion; from delusion results obscuration of memory."*
> (Krishna. *Bhagavad-Gita*, ii, 63. - Hindu tradition)

Another personal flaw is to love having more and more of the same things that other people have, only better and better things – in order to gain the approval, admiration and even envy of others. This obsession may alternatively take the form of miserliness. In its extreme form, a dominating love of pleasure results in one having no consideration for the needs of others – merely a willingness to exploit them for one's own ends. When in this state, we will be willing to act corruptly, deceitfully and mercilessly, all for the sake of gaining and enjoying the things of the world.

However, even if self-concern and addiction to pleasure have taken hold of us, there is still hope. When we are going in the wrong direction, God does not mind us making a u-turn – in fact he would be delighted. It is never too late to make a heart-felt and consistent change in our behaviour. This is where religion has its greatest appeal. Swedenborg, for example, emphasises how God can rescue us from our failings whenever we genuinely seek his help.[5] Once we do start going in the right direction, we then experience some inner development – though not as a sudden event associated with conversion of belief. Rather this would be a step-by-step process of change – attended at times by inevitably associated 'growth-pains'. For example at each stage of the process we may bemoan no longer having a particular thing, for which we had craved, but we will nevertheless more and more experience a deeper contentment by foregoing it.

*"A woman giving birth to a child has pain because her time has come;
but when her baby is born she forgets the anguish because of her joy that a child
is born into the world. So with you: Now is your time of grief, but I will see you
again and you will rejoice, and no one will take away your joy."*
(Jesus' words recorded in John 16:21-22)

Personal growth that is also spiritual growth goes beyond the issues dealt with in the personal therapy and growth movements. It involves trust and confidence in a higher spiritual power and needs to take place in several stages over a life-time.

*"The regeneration of a man, inasmuch as it is a separation and deliverance
from evils and falsities, is a particular redemption by the Lord."*
(Swedenborg. *Coronis* section 21 [7])

12. Feeling Good about Oneself

Introduction

What do we think of ourselves? Are we pleased with who we are or ashamed? Can we cope without taking someone's critical remarks about us out of all proportion? Having self-esteem means feeling good about ourselves despite not getting things right all the time. Unfortunately, some people have low self-esteem. They feel bad about themselves.

Consider the child who rushes home from school proudly telling mum or dad 'I came second in class' only to be asked about who came first. How crushed that child would feel. The harsh inner voice of low self-esteem is just like that parent. Think of the baby who is unplanned and not wanted. What a profound influence a lack of love would have as the infant develops a sense of identity and self-perception. No wonder such individuals feel they are no good and undeserving if even their own parents don't value them enough to show warmth and affection. As such individuals grow older, in their hearts they continue to feel unworthy and thus focus their thinking on their supposed inability to meet even minimum standards. As a result, they behave in negative ways that are self-defeating.

I would argue that many people with low self-esteem may not necessarily think they are 'worthless' but nevertheless they do feel as if they do not matter much and have little to offer. Youngsters who have low self-esteem give up easily at schoolwork, and do not expect they will do as well as others. Psychologists have found that a strong sense of worth goes along with being confident and assertive, having good physical health, and pleasing relationships.

Loving, close, and uninterrupted relationships within a stable family context during childhood give us the emotional grounding that is the foundation for a developing self-esteem. Also of importance are experiences of supportive relationships in adult life. Yet, despite receiving what we regard as a good upbringing some of us may feel we do not deserve to be happy and are puzzled as to where this negativity comes from.

The Unfair Judge

I would suggest the answer is something to do with the habits of thinking we have acquired during a lifetime of negative self-evaluation. Not all the causes of human behaviour can be blamed on 'nature' and 'nurture'. To my mind, there are three things that affect our lives. Firstly there is 'nature' – our constitution, for example our temperament and other aspects of our genetic makeup. Secondly, there is 'nurture' – our environment, for example the kind of home life we had as children and the limitations and opportunities inherent in our social circumstances as we develop in adulthood. And thirdly, there are the personal choices made as we live our lives, for example the choice whether or not to follow whatever our inner light is telling us. In other words, we can affect our self-esteem by what beliefs and values we choose to accept.

Thomas Edison once said:

"I haven't failed, I've found 10,000 ways that don't work"

If we interpret what we do as a failure, then it is a short jump to saying 'I am a failure'. Our feelings are greatly affected by how we think about what we do. The heart, head and hands again. Are we quick to label ourselves as undeserving? Do we think we are jinxed? Do we attribute the cause of things that go wrong to the ups and downs of normal living or do we tend to blame ourselves unfairly?

Self-labelling can be destructive just as much as discriminating against others on the basis of race, gender or social class. We may over-generalise about someone we meet on the basis of one salient fact about them. When we do this positively we draw a halo around their heads. Think of the nurses in hospitals. They are all angels are they not? But make negative conclusions about someone on the basis of their sex or race and in Britain we may be breaking the law. Unfortunately there is no law to stop us taking a judgmental approach to ourselves. Discrimination because of social groupings or age was an easy error to fall into until political consciousness has awoken us to this form of judgmental attitude. Just as we may over-generalise about certain types of people according to social stereotypes so we may over-generalise about ourselves.

If we have a poor sense of self-worth, we often experience an inner voice unfairly criticising our thoughts and actions. This voice makes snap judgments and jumps to conclusions merely on the basis of superficial information. It prevents us from trying new things and puts us down. It compares us unfavourably with other people and attributes any success we may have merely to chance. Our failures are only to be expected.

Ideas Regarding Human Nature

Some religious people have mistakenly come to equate their idea of God with this judging voice. The traditional idea for them means that since Adam's Fall everyone deserves to be condemned. These days however many people tend to assume humanity's basic goodness and resourcefulness for self-improvement. They have largely discarded the old Christian idea of original sin and no longer generally believe that mankind is inherently evil.

In my view a better idea is slightly different from both of these outlooks. This idea sees us as being born neither bad nor good. Instead, we are born with positive and negative inclinations [1]. The infant having a natural instinct for survival and for getting its needs met, wakes parents up at night by crying or screaming when hungry or uncomfortable. We recognise in the baby's ignorance of right and wrong an innocence of all blame. Although we love the baby for its charm, warmth and helplessness, at the same time neither can any credit be given for these heavenly qualities - for only as an individual gets older and becomes aware of other people in their own right, can he or she be expected to be responsible for any warmth of thought and consideration for others. In other words, culpability is to do with what we each intend and not to do with our inborn nature or our early learning – the latter two being a product not of our own choices but rather that of genetic makeup and early family environment.

I favour the view that only when we reinforce and confirm good or bad impulses – by wilfully doing what we know is right or wrong – can the spirit of truth show us to be responsible for any character traits expressed in our patterns of behaviour.

Letting Go of the Past

Part of the problem of low self-esteem may be when we are not letting go of the past. Colin, a thirty-six year old professional actor was well known on the London stage and had appeared in several TV drama series. He was married to Cynthia who worked in accountancy. The couple had no children. Despite his professional success, Colin had periods of low mood, even at times thinking about suicide, although he had never intended this course of action. These bouts of depressed mood happened between professional engagements and so his career had not so far been harmed. However, he had been receiving antidepressant medication prescribed by his GP who also recently recommended personal counselling.

Colin always avoided asking for favours because he did not think he deserved them. If anybody complimented his work he was very embarrassed. When a youngster, he had been told by his parents on occasions that he had let them down because of his naughty behaviour or had been a disappointment to them because of his school exam results. Being an only child, he had no yardstick with which to compare himself. It had never occurred to him that the opinion of his parents was wrong, for like all small children he took on board what they had to say as gospel truth.

However, now as an adult he could begin to identify the messages that he received all those years ago. His therapist helped him to re-visit the past in imagination. He learned how to say more helpful and reassuring things to the imagined child that was himself, and to acknowledge that he was then only a child and now knew better regarding his parents' character. In addition, he practised pretending to point out to his parents their unfair criticism of him. The result of several sessions of this kind of bolstering and strengthening of his self-image resulted in a lift in mood. Although sometimes he did relapse into his old patterns of thought, nevertheless in general he came to see himself in a different light as okay – someone who could hold his head up high.

Tackling Undermining Relationships

Colin had married a woman who tended to nag him and put him down. Given his fragile ego, it was no wonder he had previously felt drained and discontented whenever she picked on him. It was as if he had needed someone in his life to confirm what he had come to think of himself i.e. as someone unworthy. He never appreciated that he did not always need to take what she said so personally. He came to realise that many of those occasions when she was negative towards him, actually said more about her and her state of mind than about himself e.g. her unreasonable expectations of him when she was tired and stressed by her job. He need no longer feel undermined by her. He decided to try to get his wife to work on their communication together.

His therapist also asked him to focus on his strengths rather than his failings. This he found very difficult, as he had assumed that he had few positive qualities. Of course, people rarely openly tell you what they value about you and so we have to guess sometimes as to what they like in us. However, he did start to think about what he liked about himself, regardless of his achievements.

If our relationship with someone is undermining our sense of self-worth then we need to do something about it. If the problem is our spouse we could perhaps try marital counselling with a view to improving the relationship. Colin had resolved to himself that if his wife did not respond positively to this serious opportunity for change then he would consider whether to leave her to find another person in his life to encourage him and be more upbeat. The couple had no children who could have been hurt by such a move.

Likewise, if our relationship with our God is undermining us then we could perhaps consider whether our image of God is at fault and needs ditching in favour of a truer one that makes more sense.

God's Assessment of Us

We may ask how could God's spirit - being the source of love and wisdom - create anything bad in us and want to denounce anyone as unworthy? I would answer this by saying "No, anything that is bad, is created by me when I knowingly choose a life that is contrary to my values and principles." It is I and not God who may judge myself as worthless and in doing so condemn myself to a guilty verdict. Of course in this way I would be my own worst enemy.

Just because I have a certain failing, I may mistakenly see my whole character as bad. I am quite likely to do this if I have come to believe that one should be thoroughly competent, adequate and achieving in all possible respects to consider oneself worthwhile. We may project this self-judgmental attitude on to our image of God as if he were an angry judge. The Old Testament Bible appears to be full of such pictures. However, the New Testament reveals a deeper truth. Jesus pointed out to his listeners that if the birds of the air who neither sow seeds nor reap are taken care of, how much more does God care for as worthy in our own right.

I follow Swedenborg's line that like a good parent, God actually seeks to boost us up and focus on the potential good things we can do. In other words the image of the God I can believe in is one of compassion, mercy, and forgiveness – a God who never gets angry, never wants us to suffer, never wants anything bad to befall us.

The Divine Working in Us.

I believe that spiritually sensitive people may often experience a sense of inspiration and enlightenment due to the divine inflowing into their lives.[2] I believe that this can become available to everyone, for we all receive this influx and have the potential to grow as people and reach this level of spiritual maturity. The question of self-esteem becomes less important to us as we realise that we are all worthy to receive this spiritual force. This is the spirit of God working in and by us as we get on with the business of daily living. This is not a million miles away from the position of humanistic and existential psychologists who tend to think that only a humane, non-dogmatic, and non-sectarian form of religiousness – the essence of which is genuine feeling – is a source of purpose and meaning conducive to the realisation of our potential.

Psychoanalysis attempts to explain what it regards as a primitive irrational orientation to religion as having its origin in our helpless fears in confronting the dangerous forces of nature. In so speaking of religion as effectively an illusion, it is talking about the way we respond to these fears with guilt. We may attempt to appease a divine being who, in our limited notion of him, keeps dominant control and power over people and nature.

However, even Freud wrote that the image of God is important for the individual to help with self-identity, and prevent insecurity and self-absorption. He said that the 'ego ideal' aspect of the mind is a vital component of the personality and its development.[3] By ego ideal he means rules for good behaviour, and standards of excellence towards which the person must strive. It is basically what the child's parents approve of or value.

Worthy of God's Love

I would like to mention God's esteem for us despite what I believe to be our fallen state with inherited self-centred tendencies. None of us starts off life in any way guilty of making these tendencies actual. However, even if we were to, I believe that we would all nevertheless be worthy to receive God's love and blessings. This is because I strongly believe that God sees us as we can be and loves us as we are. For Swedenborg this view is exemplified in Jesus Christ as incarnate God willing to face human evil in the world and suffer at its hands for all our sakes. We are all worthy to receive the uplifting spirit of the divine.

Humility

The spiritually-minded person has a profound sense of humility. Such a person does not experience self-pride, but rather appreciates the worthiness of actions inspired by and filled with divine spirit.

When we come to examine ourselves honestly, we come to realise that most of what we do comes from a mixed motive. I suspect that no good thing I have ever done has been completely driven by an unselfish purity of purpose. The essence of the spiritual attitude is to accept the need for a new direction – a spiritual rebirth – because of an acceptance that, of ourselves, we possess no goodness – only acting on what is inspired in us in the moment by God.

> *"Count your rectitude as foolishness, know your cleverness to be stupidity"*
> (Lao Tse. *Tao Teb King*, xlv)

> *"The beginning of philosophy, at least with those who lay hold of it as they ought and enter by the door, is the consciousness of their own feebleness and incapacity in respect of necessary things."*
> (Epictetus. *Dissertation*, ii,II,I.)

But we need not castigate ourselves for our self-oriented tendencies. When confessing my errors and failings, I realise that with the divine presence within me I can do better, for I was created as an image of God. Feeling good about what I do is very different from feeling I am good. I believe that from myself alone I can do nothing that is purely altruistic, yet God working within me can originate much that is truly good through me. We can humbly acknowledge that all that we achieve that is good in our lives is due to a spiritual force which is greater than we ourselves. Paradoxically the result of this is that we experience a greater sense of worth. We see that all the worthwhile things we do are a result of being a willing channel for the power of divine love and wisdom.

> *"No one ever possesses good or truth that is his own but…all good and truth flow in from the Lord… Nevertheless it seems as though that good or truth is his own, and the reason for this is that these may be made over to him as his own until the time when he enters that state in which he may know, then acknowledge, and at length believe that they are not his but the Lord's."*
> (Swedenborg. *Arcana Coelestia* section 4151 [3])

13. Asking for Help

Why We Need to Ask for Help

Life can pile on too many problems at once. Circumstances can suddenly change. Anyone can lose their livelihood, or suffer a prolonged or difficult illness. The first step is to admit to ourselves when we actually do need help.

Asking for help can be difficult. The inclination to delay is strong. We often hope that the problem will resolve itself. We say that we are "fine" and that we are in control. However, often problems do not go away unless we help them along.

If we need something, why would we not simply ask for it? If we do not ask, how can we expect to get any advice or assistance?

Reasons for Not Asking

There may be embarrassment discussing a personal matter with friends or family. "I ought to be able to manage my own life without troubling others with my difficulties." Is it pride that gets in the way of asking? Yet we are humble enough to seek expert help from an accountant or lawyer.

No one likes feeling criticised. Is our reluctance to do with having to admit some failing or flaw and feeling ashamed? "What will they think of me if I ask for help?" "I might not be promoted if my boss thinks I can't do the job."

We may assume we are too unimportant or unlikeable for anyone to want to bother going out of his or her way to do us a service. "No-one will want to help me."

Alternatively, we might think that no one would understand our problem or that no help could be available given the enormity of the need. "My problems are unsolvable." "My life is in far too great a mess to be saved."

Asking for help is dangerous because actually accepting help may well be no easy option. It will probably involve our co-operation with the help given - complying with the new exercise regime, debt repayment scheme or whatever. We are scared getting help could mean too much effort from ourselves to give up what we have found comfortable. The problem needs a different solution to the too easy one we had been pursuing like for example engaging in comfort eating or retail therapy.

How to Ask

If we do get round to asking for help, it is useful to be clear what we think we need. Whether we need advice, encouragement, or practical help, we need to ask for it specifically.

At the same time, it is sensible to be flexible. What someone offers may be unexpected. Therefore, we need to be ready to explore alternatives. People tend to feel uncomfortable about helping the unprepared or the narrow-minded. This means being willing to listen carefully to what they suggest.

Whom to Ask

I saw a woman walking into a council refuse tip to get rid of a long fluorescent light tube. She unfortunately tripped over and dropped the tube that exploded in a puff of smoke. It looked and sounded dramatic. Her elderly friend was following on behind and at that moment, seeing the prostrate woman and hearing the explosion, she exclaimed 'Oh God, God' and rushed forward. This friend may not have been religious but was she not asking for God's help without even realising it? Perhaps he did answer her prayer for although she was a bit shocked, the fallen woman got up and dusted herself down. It turned out that she had suffered no injury.

If the help needed is beyond the capability of loved ones or friends, we may decide to ask God for assistance.

Psychologists have studied two factors in religious attitude called 'extrinsic' and 'intrinsic' religious orientations.[1] The former is being disposed to use religion for one's own benefit. The latter, on the other hand, is finding religion to be what really lies behind the whole approach to life.

It is possible to score highly or lowly on both factors. Those who score highly *only* on the 'extrinsic' orientation can be said to be not inwardly spiritual. They go through the ritual of prayer and worship. In their hearts, they do not love to think about the teachings of their religion nor about the right way to live. Their main motive for falling in with religious belief is for their own benefit as it can provide a sense of belonging, respect from others, and comfort. We can ask for help for our problems but if we pray *only* for ourselves how can God hear such prayers?

On the other hand, there are religious people who are not hypocritical, who are genuine in efforts to follow their religion, and who do love their religious teaching for its own sake. Whether or not they score highly on the 'extrinsic' scale, they do score highly on the 'intrinsic' one. Their spiritual awareness moves them to pray humbly for help in times of trouble but not in any way to the detriment of others or of moral values. Their concern is not just for themselves. They have charity in their hearts, religious belief in their heads that they follow in the work of their hands. Not only do they pray for the unfortunate, the troubled and those who suffer, but they also ask God how they could be of assistance – no easy thing to say because the answer may involve an element of personal sacrifice. Unlike some religious people, those with such spiritual attitudes tend not to be prejudiced, dogmatic and ethnocentric in their social attitudes.

Motivation behind Prayer

One morning David, a man with problems, was walking in a solitary place as usual. [2] He was thinking about what he was trying to do off his own bat to save himself from his personal difficulties and failings. He then realised that all his attempts had been ineffective and his religious worship and pleas for help were in vain. It came to him that it was self-interest behind his devotions rather than any respect for the wisdom of God. It was his own happiness and not the will of God that had pre-occupied his heart. He saw he had never done anything for God, only for himself. He stayed in this state of mind for three days and, feeling depressed, he attempted to pray but found no heart to engage in this and felt the spirit of God had quite left him. He felt desolate as if nothing in heaven or earth could make him happy.

After nearly half an hour of trying to pray, he began to sense a change. He describes this as a totally new view of the divine and he says he experienced a state of inward joy and was so delighted with the excellence of God that he was swallowed up by him and had no thought of his own problems. Later, he was amazed that he had not previously dropped what he described as his own contrivances and had not simply followed God's way.

Speaking with God

"Invoking God himself, not with external speech, but with the soul itself, extending ourselves in prayer to him, since we shall then be able to pray to him properly, when we approach by ourselves alone to the alone"
(Plotinus. *Ennead*, v,1,6 – Ancient Greek philosophy.)

When praying with a sincere heart it is useful to speak specifically about the issues that we require help with. We could then ask God to give us new purpose, a healthier frame of mind in facing our troubles, or more light on how we can better serve our family and community. Perhaps praying is something we have rarely done before. So how can one go about this?[3]

If our idea of God is of one who is all-powerful – power to change anything anywhere – we may still forget this and voice our doubts whether he is capable of helping us. If our idea of God is of one who is all-knowing - knowing everything about everything - we may nevertheless assume he needs reminding of what we need. If our idea of God is of one who is all-loving – pure compassion and concern for all creation – we may still think he needs prompting before wanting to do something for us.

We may feel that God is not answering our prayers. True, we may not be hearing a voice answering but there will always be a response. Sometimes we may not notice it because it is not what we have expected. As we try to pray for help we may realise something about our own attitude e.g. like David, that it is too oriented towards self rather than towards any concern for anyone else. Already the prayer is being answered without our noticing.

If we do not ask, then we do not get an answer – but the answer may not be what we would have wanted! Actually, many inwardly religious people believe that divine power can spiritually help all people, no matter what terrible state they have got themselves into.

"He who believes in God says also within himself, 'With God's help I will overcome it'; and so he makes supplication, and gets help. This is not denied to anyone, but is given to him, because the Lord, from his divine Love, is in the continual endeavour to reform and regenerate man, ...and this constant endeavour of the Lord comes into effect, when the man truly desires it, and makes an effort for it."
(Swedenborg. *Charity* 203)

14. Learning to Trust

Introduction

We may feel uneasy and wary of other people. The suspicion is that they will seize on our mistakes and try to make out that anything which goes wrong is all our own fault. Perhaps we feel irritated by trivial things they do because we suspect that they are trying to annoy us. Alternatively, maybe we feel that they are liable to cheat us if we are not alert to stopping this.

Having a distrust of the world can be unpleasant because we continually need to check out if people are doing us down. In addition, being distrustful of others, we do not easily form personal relationships; for to get close to someone would involve putting ourselves in a vulnerable position where we might get hurt. We do not want to risk them betraying us if we start to depend on them. Yet keeping ourselves to ourselves we feel lonely.

Possible Causes of Suspicion

Many of us who are 'naturally suspicious' and have difficulty trusting others, have grown up in families that we experienced as a bit hazardous. Someone in the family may have ridiculed any signs of sensitivity or weakness in our make-up, our parents or siblings may have lied to us and cheated us, or they may have physically assaulted us. If any of these things happened, we soon learned that the world is a 'dog eat dog' sort of place where one must be tough to survive.

We may have got into the habit of looking closely at what others say or do, watching for threats to what we are used to, or for threats to our good name. The result is that we probably just end up seeing what we are looking for. After all, not everyone is caring and reliable. Often we can read what someone says either way because the meaning behind their communication is often sufficiently unclear. Yet, we can blinker ourselves to any signs of consideration or concern by only looking for intimidation, manipulation or malice. By being over-watchful for indications of deceit, we miss any possibility of noticing the other person's good intentions.

Towards Solutions

One way to learn how to trust others is to try to stop being negative and defensive with them. Unfortunately being negative can provoke the very attitude in them that we were expecting in the first place. This is when we make mountains out of molehills, or are quick to counterattack if criticised, or bear grudges when wronged, or are unforgiving of insults, or we jealously question - without justification - our partner's movements. Our own hostile behaviour causes a self-fulfilling prophecy. The solution, when in a hole, is to stop digging. One alternative to hole digging – instead of being quick to blame others or find fault in them – is to be more honest with them regarding our own short-comings and the extent to which we might be contributing to the problem.

Spiritual Perspective

I would say that the key to a trusting attitude is to look for the good and concern in those we encounter and deal with the faults of others as gently as with our own.[1] We are in a state of peace inside only when we are seeking or finding peace around us. Looking for the good in others may mean, for example, making an effort to understand the other person's point of view. By becoming more aware of where he or she is coming from, we then give ourselves a better chance more accurately to distinguish between innocent remarks, fair criticism, things said only in anger of the moment, and hostile put-downs.

Looking for the good in others may mean our noticing the spirit of humanity around us. If we cannot see this caring spirit in our family members and acquaintances, we can instead perhaps notice it in people working in the caring professions, charity volunteers or local community workers as well as famous individuals like Mother Theresa and Francis of Assisi.

Looking for the good in others when we usually look for the bad in them requires an effort of will. We do not often find the idea of 'will' in modern psychology. One exception is in psychosynthesis psychotherapy created by Roberto Assagioli.[2] According to Assagioli everyone can have, or has had, the experience of freely willing but possibly not with full awareness or understanding. He said that people vary in the extent they explore, develop and use their will to develop their life.

Having a new heart is a crucial part of our spiritual growth. As I have already indicated, to my mind, the source of such a new heart of altruism is the God of love, who has a concern for the whole human race. Such a heart means a sympathetic approach to other people, *not* because they happen to agree with our views about things, *nor* because of any exchange of flattery or reciprocal scratching of backs. A charitable heart is looking for the good in others and valuing them for the potential good they can do.

It is also treating others as oneself. This is universal advice.

Jesus said:

> *"So in everything, do to others what you would have them do to you,*
> *for this sums up the Law and the Prophets."*
> (Matthew: 7:12)

The Buddha said:

> *"Hurt not others with that which pains yourself"*
> (*Udana*, v, 18. – Buddhist tradition)

Jainism says:

> *"Treat others as you would be treated yourself."*
> (*Yogashastra*, ii, 20 – Hindu tradition)

It is even possible for those of us who are a bit mean-spirited to learn to treat others generously and even learn to return good for ill.

Although the possibility of such a new heart that amounts to loving one's enemies may sound doubtful to some of us, nevertheless we can actually tap into and take into ourselves a powerful spiritual force – a love that genuinely is concerned for the happiness and welfare of all. The religious message is that when we try to act as a channel for divine love in our lives, it will become easier to learn to trust other people. If we start treating others as themselves worthy of having good points and being capable of treating us with care and respect, then we will find it easier to put our trust in them.

> *"People in whom charity is present think nothing else than good of the*
> *neighbour and speak nothing but good, and this not for their own sake or*
> *that of him with whom they seek to curry favour… (They) stir up nothing*
> *but goods and truths; and things that are evil and false they excuse."*
> (Swedenborg. *Arcana Coelestia* section 1088 [2])

15. Attaining Peace of Mind

Worry

Are you a happy-go-lucky sort of person or one who gets uptight about things? It is right to be concerned if we lose our job, if our children are ill, or if we are having relationship problems. For then we are stimulated to try to do something about it. However, the problem of anxious worry is when our thoughts about something go round in circles without getting anywhere. We may also fail to find peace of mind because we are pre-occupied with things although they may never happen or later turn out not so bad as we had imagined.

If a mother's love is withdrawn perhaps due to illness or family turmoil, it is understandable that the child may grow feeling emotionally insecure, anxious and thus easily worried.

However, in general, anxiety is a common element in personal problems. In extreme cases of fear, spiritual growth may be delayed as long as rationality and inner freedom are adversely affected: love opens the interiors of the mind but fear closes them.

A Problem Shared

When we are worried, it often helps to talk with someone who appreciates how we feel and can possibly help put things in perspective. The other person might make comments that help us see things from a different angle. Our friend, colleague or whoever, can keep us in touch with reality, so our fears are not exaggerated. Although we need *not* take on board everything the person suggests, he or she can only help as long as we carefully listen to what is said. If instead we ask the same person over and over again for reassurance, this unfortunately can drive that person to distraction and we gain no benefit.

Normality of Anxiety

We speak of the 'born worrier' and it is probably true that there is an inherited disposition towards anxiety that affects some of us more than others. However, the experience of some anxiety is universal because it goes hand in hand with the experience of daily life that throws up all sorts of challenges. The fact that we have a strong desire for certain things means that we are likely to feel anxious if anything turns up to prevent us having them.

Three Types of Anxiety

In general, according to Swedenborg, there are three kinds of things we love. Thus, there are three different types of anxiety when something threatens what we love. Firstly, there is wanting something for the sake of self – such as financial wealth, social status and feeling accepted. We may feel anxious if we become ill and our health is threatened.

A second category is concern for others – for instance caring about the common welfare of our family, friends or community. We may feel worried for instance for hungry people if there is a famine or for someone we know well who is in dire straits. We can immediately focus social concern on someone we know or experience a global concern for those we have never met.

A third type is to do with principles and values that we hold dear. We may admire the principle of justice or long for something we highly value such as leading a productive and useful life. In the music of his late sonatas and quartets, Ludwig van Beethoven revealed spiritual depths. For me such music expresses the ideal of selfless love that finds its highest expression in the value of human fraternity and reconciliation. We may feel deeply anxious without realising why. This is often due to a problem with this third kind of love. One example is when we no longer feel in harmony with what we truly value. We may fear we are losing something precious in our life – an aspiration for all that is good and wise perhaps.

Some people doubt whether there is any spiritual power to protect them from the unknown, or whether there is any supernatural existence for life to continue beyond the grave. Given the inevitability of death it is perhaps understandable if they worry about their health or about their safety. Yet common sense tells us there is no point in worrying about something we cannot do anything about. Unless thinking about a difficulty prompts us to effective action, worry about it is pointless. This means accepting that there is not a lot in life over which we ourselves can have foresight, let alone control.

Accepting Life's Uncertainties

We all need to learn to live with uncertainty and this can be unsettling. No one can say for sure what the weather may be like in a week's time or that they won't get run over by a bus tomorrow. Some people say that ours is an age of anxiety, a time of upheaval of standards and values, and of painful insecurity. This state of change in the world can only add to our feeling unsure of what the next day will bring.

However, some of us seem to believe that worrying about something in the future can make a difference. The assumption is, if something is unsafe or scary, one should be very concerned about it and keep thinking about whether or not it will happen. Jesus directly addressed the futility of fretting in this way when he advised his listeners not to worry about the next day as it will have enough worries of its own and he said that there is no need to add to the troubles each day brings (Matthew 6:34). In other words live in the present and deal with real things happening.

Helpful Coincidences

A young woman patient of Carl Gustav Jung's was proving very difficult to help in therapy because she was keeping her personal feelings to herself only conversing on an intellectual level. She had had a dream in which someone had given her a golden scarab – a costly piece of jewellery. While she was telling Jung about this dream, he heard something behind him gently tapping on the window. He turned round and saw that it was a large flying insect knocking against the window-pane in an apparent effort to get into the dark room. This seemed to him to be very strange. He opened the window immediately and caught the insect in the air as it flew in. It was a scarabaeid beetle (*Cetonia aurata*) whose gold-green colour most nearly resembles that of a golden scarab. He handed it to his patient with the words, "Here is your scarab." This moving experience broke the ice of her intellectual resistance and we are told treatment continued with satisfactory results.

Carl Jung gives this as an example of what he calls 'synchronicity'.[1] This notion was his answer to the puzzle of why people sometimes experience meaningful coincidences in their lives that are inexplicable and not due to chance. At first this sounds a bit like the magical beliefs of so-called primitive people for whom no accident, change in the weather or the health of the villagers, is ever thought to be attributable to natural causes. Everything is somehow due to magical influence. Jung does not go this far. Nevertheless, he does say that synchronicity is one of the factors in life along with natural causes. It is relevant when we are trying to fathom our experience of any purposeful trends in our affairs. The synchronous experience is said to occur when two kinds of reality (i.e. the inner and outer) intersect.

Divine Providence

I think we can be more specific regarding such experiences. Swedenborg writes that there is a divine providence that is quietly looking after our deepest needs. [2] It hides itself but we might detect it when later we notice things working out for the best. Only later, if we reflect on what has happened to us, may we possibly comprehend that various separate strands of our life have been knit together. For example, we might later appreciate how we have been nurtured deep down, how the mess and muddle we make of our own lives has been cleaned up, and how new and interesting paths for us to follow have been illuminated.

It is often impossible to assess from our limited perspective whether an event is good or bad. There is an ancient Taoist parable [3] that tells of an old man and his son who lived alone in poor conditions. Their only possession of value was a horse. One day, the horse ran away. The neighbours came by to offer sympathy, telling the old man how unlucky he was.

'How do you know?' asked the old man.

The following day the horse returned, bringing with it several wild horses, which the old man and his son locked inside their gate. This time the neighbours hurried over to congratulate the old man on his good fortune.

'How do you know?' asked the old man.

The next thing that happened was that his son tried to ride one of the wild horses but fell off and broke his leg. The neighbours were quick to tell the old man that this was a disastrous turn of events.

'How do you know?' asked the old man.

Soon after, the army came through, press-ganging young men into service to fight a battle far away. All the local young men were taken – except the old man's son, because his leg was broken.

Some notion of God as the provider can be seen in the presence of scientific laws that keep the universe in order and us along with it. One example is the way the planets follow an expected path around the sun. Another is the predictable result of combining certain chemicals together. The person of faith says that divine providence is all-knowing and all-powerful. This is God's hands at work. Being also all-loving, God wants to, and does, have involvement with the smallest detail of all our lives. This is the heart-felt compassion motivating all his actions.

I believe divine activity stops total mayhem and complete disorder that would otherwise result from human folly. I am not saying catastrophes never happen. However, this providential and healing power helps us pull through our troubles and distress. Religious people call this inexplicable thing God's foresight and spirit.

" *I tell you, do not worry about your life, what you will eat or drink; or about your body, what you will wear. Is not life more important than food, and the body more important than clothes? Look at the birds of the air; they do not sow or reap or store away in barns, and yet your heavenly Father feeds them. Are you not much more valuable than they? Who of you by worrying can add a single hour to his life?*"
(Matthew 6:25-27)

"Weary not yourself concerning the affairs of the day, nor be anxious overmuch about your house and estate."
(*The Teaching of Ptah-hoteb*, xi Ancient Egyptian philosophy)

Preserving Human Freedom

If God is active in the world why does he hide this activity from us at the time? We do not see it and, even afterwards, when he is able to show an inkling of it, we may put it down to chance events or lucky coincidences. Some speak of fate but do not know what is meant by this. The way I understand it is if we could directly see God's hands at work looking after us, mending and healing rifts, providing unexpected juxtapositions of circumstances that lead to happy outcomes, giving us answers to problems, and inspiring creative ideas, then why would we take any responsibility for doing anything ourselves for the greater good?

I believe the workings of providence are secret to prevent compelling our belief and so stopping our inner freedom. God does not want us to be robots following something like a computer program in the way we lead our lives. He knows that only by our actual choosing to co-operate with his leading can we receive his spiritual gifts. Hence the coincidental events that appear to occur by chance but are said actually to be his hands at work.

God has a wise head for like a sensible parent he permits us freedom to make mistakes whilst learning the lessons of life that will help with our character development and future happiness. At the same time, he secretly provides us with inspiration and enlightenment that will serve this purpose, although to all appearances we are going through misfortune and difficulty.

I believe that we can learn to put our trust in God to provide for our deeper needs. Those of us, who put our trust in this higher power, feel a quiet confidence and contentment and accept that, despite all the traumas we may undergo, he is in charge and is providing for us. If so, why should we fret and be anxious. All will be well in the end as long as we play our part.

Peace of Mind

Many people know of the serenity prayer: -

"God grant me the serenity to accept the things I cannot change; courage to change the things I can; and wisdom to know the difference."

We experience peace of mind when we never allow ourselves to go to the extreme in doing things for self but rather contentedly allow ourselves to be carried along in the 'stream of divine providence' making the best of our opportunities. For when the love of self no longer rules our hearts, then we rise above our worries concerning the transient things of the world.

Those are in the stream of Providence who put their trust in the divine and attribute all things to Him; and … those are not in the stream of Providence who trust in themselves alone and attribute all things to themselves… Be it known also that insofar as anyone is in the stream of Providence, so far he is in a state of peace.
(Swedenborg. *Arcana Coelestia* Section 8478 [4])

16. Dealing with Death

Common Attitudes

Across history and the world's religions, mankind has not generally seen death as an end to life and so we have been encouraged not to fear it. Yet, to watch someone die can be an upsetting experience. How will we survive the loss of this person we love? The occurrence of a death reminds us of our own bodily mortality. Especially when a young person dies, it is an unwanted reminder that not every dream of a long, happy life comes true.

In differing degrees, many of us do not cope well with the idea of death. Perhaps we do not share the Christian belief in resurrection and a heavenly afterlife, and would rather be anywhere than at a funeral. People often avoid speaking the very word 'death' directly and instead use euphemisms such as 'passed away', 'gone', or 'no longer with us'. Some people are even ready to spend lots of money to try to postpone death or ask that a specialist organisation keep their corpse in a deeply frozen state in case one day it is possible for them to revive it. The thought of our own body disintegrating after we die may feel too much to bear.

Indications of Another Realm

Most people will certainly not want to think about death if they imagine it to mean total oblivion and nothingness. However, according to hospice staff and others who provide end-of-life care, dying people sometimes sense another realm beyond our material world.

In addition, evidence for life after death comes from many people having had visions when their life has been in peril. Reports of their experiences show noticeable similarities although each is unique. A young man was skating on the local reservoir and fell through the ice. As he approached hypothermia, he could hardly move. He went down in silence his lifeless arms floating above his head. He then stopped feeling afraid and actually started to feel warm. Feeling at peace and physically comfortable, he felt he was being drawn backwards down a long, dark tube, and sucked past a wall of spongy black cotton. Over his shoulder, he saw what looked like the sun having a soft yellow glow.

Dr Moody and other researchers into this type of experience call it the 'near death experience' (NDE). [1] He presents a composite picture gathered from many similar accounts.

"A man is dying and as he reaches the point of greatest physical distress he hears himself pronounced dead by his doctor. He begins to hear an uncomfortable noise – a loud ringing or buzzing – and at the same time feels himself moving very rapidly through a long dark tunnel. After this, he suddenly finds himself outside his own physical body but still in the immediate physical environment and he sees his own body from a distance as though he is a spectator. He watches the resuscitation attempt from this unusual vantage point and is in a state of emotional upheaval. After a while he collects himself and becomes more accustomed to his new condition. He notices that he still has a body but one of a very different nature and with very different powers from the physical body he has left behind. Soon other things begin to happen. Others come to meet and help him. He glimpses the spirits of relatives and friends who have already died and a loving warm spirit of light of a kind he had never encountered before appears before him. This being asks him a question non-verbally to make him evaluate his life and helps him by showing him a panoramic instantaneous playback of the major events of his life. At some point he finds himself approaching some sort of barrier or border apparently representing the limit between earthly life and the next life. But he finds that he must go back to earth ; that the time for his death has not yet come At this point he resists, for by now he is taken up by his experiences in the afterlife and does not want to return. He is overwhelmed by intense feelings of joy love and peace. Despite his attitude, he somehow reunites with his physical body and lives. Later he tries to tell others but he has trouble doing so. In the first place he can find no human words adequate to describe these unearthly episodes. He also finds that others scoff so he stops telling other people. Still the experience affects his life profoundly and especially his views about death and its relationship to life."

The NDE is like *neither* a dream *nor* a so-called hallucination because there seems to be a common pattern seen by many people. These people often tell of the following: the appearance of a bright light, encountering others such as deceased relatives and friends and being taken back - like in a video replay - through all the important incidents in their life.

Swedenborg's Extraordinary Experiences

These accounts are in line with the reports of Swedenborg given in a huge volume of meticulously written-up testimony regarding his own unusual personal experiences. His visions spanned the last 27 years of his life. He discovered he could see, hear and feel in a non-physical dimension that he termed 'the spiritual world'. I can readily accept that this spirit realm is the dimension of life into which we all become conscious after the death of our natural body. He claimed an extraordinary gift – of not only seeing spirits and hearing their voices speaking but also being seen and heard as to his own spirit even whilst, at the same time, present with others in the material world. He insisted that what he saw and heard in the spirit world came to him not in dreams but in 'the highest state of wakefulness'. He claimed to be able to converse with spirits and learn an astonishing amount about the next life and the laws according to which it operates, from living experience as well as instruction. He described these extraordinary visions and spiritual laws in many of his published books.

The Spiritual World

Those people reporting on their NDE's say that subjective time does not match earthly time as observed by nurses and medics. This parallels Swedenborg's account of time in the spirit realm. [2] In the spiritual world, like here on earth, things are said to happen in progressive sequence. There, the passing of time reflects our state of mind rather than any objective criteria in the physical universe such as the working of a clock. We are all familiar with time dragging when we are bored and flying past when we are fully absorbed in something. He said the angels do not have any concept of clock time, though they are conscious of the changing and succession of states of life. Likewise, many mystics have reported this experience of timelessness.

Those having a NDE were still physically alive even though they reported out-of-body experiences. This would often involve the person seeming to rise in the air and looking down in the hospital on the medical team working on their physical body. Such an experience suggests that the spirit of a person can be independent of the physical body yet still have conscious sensation. This ties in with Swedenborg's report that in the spiritual world, we live in a spirit body after having left our physical body behind. This spirit body is perfect and whole, regardless of what condition the physical body might have been in at the time of death. The individual's appearance gradually changes to harmonise with and reflect the quality of the spirit – good or bad. The spirit people say that they enjoy the same senses as they enjoyed whilst alive in the physical world; for example, they see as before, and they hear and speak as before, only now using their spirit body.

Our surroundings in the spirit realm are said to appear just as solid and real and are filled with familiar things such as minerals, flora and fauna of all kinds, with houses, communities, schools, recreation areas and so on. Nevertheless, as with time, there is no objectively fixed space as such – only its appearance. All journeys in the spiritual world effectively mirror changes of the state of mind of the person. The apparent distance between two spirits reflects the degree of empathy and similarity of character between them.

When we first die, those friends and relatives, who retain the loving attitude to us they had when living in the world, are close by to meet us. People experiencing NDE's also report meeting dead relatives; also suggesting life continues for all beyond the grave. It is noticeable that those with NDE's are more likely, as a result, to believe in an afterlife.

I can accept that individuals in the after-life of spirit have desire, intention, thought and reflection as before their bodily death. For example, one who liked academic study, reads and writes as before. When individuals pass from being part of the physical world into the spirit world, it is like passing from one place into another, carrying with them all things that they are in themselves as a person; so that after death of the body, one will have lost nothing that is inwardly part of oneself.

Reports of Mediums

Various mediums have spoken about what spirits have told them concerning the realm of spirits. [3] There are striking similarities between these accounts and Swedenborg's writings as follows:-

- The soul body exists.
- Spirits clothe themselves with thought.
- Time means nothing.
- Environment appears created by thought.
- We gravitate to the shared environment of like-minded spirits.
- We revert to the bodily appearance of our early twenties.
- There is a self-evaluation involving how we lived life on earth.
- One's inner character does not change because of death.

- Punishment is only part of a purification process.
- There is no procreation.
- There are useful occupational and similar interests; albeit at a higher level.
- There is an upper Astral akin to heaven.
- There is no pain or alarm during the dying process.
- Because of the similarity of experience to life, new arrivals do not at first notice they are dead.

The world's religions have also pointed to the immortality of the human spirit.

> *"The whole body of spiritual substance progresses without a pause; the whole body of material substance suffers decay without intermission".*
> (*Lieh Tse* – Taoist tradition)

> *"The worldly existence is in the end death and disappearance, and of the spiritual existence, in the end, that of a soul of the righteous is un-decaying, immortal, and undisturbed."*
> (*Menog-I Khrad*, xl, 29-30 – Zoroastrianism tradition)

The Emerging Self

As I understand it, the spiritual world forces no-one after death to be something that he or she is not. When we are alive in the body on earth, our outer thoughts are busy when we are with other people, or engaged in some action. However, our inner thoughts come from what we are really feeling when we are alone at home. In the next life, the values that deep down rule our hearts come to the surface and unrelated feelings, pretences and difficulties become dormant. We each get more in touch with our true selves, and all other spirits see the genuine nature of everyone's character; whether this is selfish and destructive or caring and creative. In other words, our inner feelings and desires determine our destiny. You really are what you choose to be, and pretending to be something other than what you really are becomes increasingly difficult to maintain.

Swedenborg reports that after we awake in the spirit realm we may find ourselves in some kind of living environment – often one we have been familiar with on earth. This gradually changes, beginning more and more to reflect the quality of our own thoughts and feelings. It may be a room in a very beautiful house or an untidy shed. It is in fact a projection of our inner state. What one sees in the spiritual world is a reflection of different aspects of one's own true inner self. As we are all different there are many kinds of living accommodation and environment.

"In my Father's house are many rooms; if it were not so, I would have told you. I am going there to prepare a place for you."
(John 14,2)

"Vauna, you glorious lord, I have entered your loft house, your house with its thousand portals...Bring me to dwell in that abiding city."
(*Rig Veda*, vii, 88, 5-7. – Hindu tradition)

The goodness or otherwise of one's character shines more clearly in the spirit realm than in our material world where people, who do not know us well, see only our outward persona and where our style of living is more apparent. This illumination is illustrated in Near Death Experiences by the frequently mentioned encounter with a 'being of light' and of a life evaluation.

We love one thing more than anything. It colours all our life. It could be for example a love of being useful, of the spiritual ideas we believe to be true, of having power over others, or of being popular and well liked. This is our underlying longing that is the essence of our true character. Many of our desires arise from this basic love. We are most likely to reveal our true selves by our actions when we do not think others are observing us.

In the other life there is a gradual change for an individual, towards higher or lower qualitative levels of existence. Those who are essentially self-centred and uncaring of others slowly begin to show their real character, and thus begin to mix in the company of other lower-level spirits, creating, together with them, a hellish environment. On the other hand, those who are of better character and more concerned for others rise to a higher level, together with other angelic spirits, creating a heavenly sphere. For this reason, although family ties are not necessarily broken after death, only the ties of real affection survive where there is like-mindedness and thus a sharing of a spiritual environment is possible.

"You are what your deep driving desire is. As your desire is, so is your will. As your will is, so is your deed. As your deed is, so is your destiny."
(*The Upanishads* – Hindu tradition)

Preparing for the Next Realm

Whether or not we believe in life after death, we can all be afraid of death and dying to some extent. Perhaps we fear a lack of control over the process of deterioration that precedes death – whether it will involve pain or loss of dignity. But just as there can be no spring without the cold of winter that comes before it – so the pain of suffering can be seen to precede the triumph of new life.

Death for us is eternity knocking at the door. Perhaps, an avoidance of thinking of it is due to our realising that we are not living now as we would want to live to eternity. The trouble is that often we are unwilling to allow what is bad in us to die. A reminder of the reality of death is a wake-up call to discard the trivial and prioritise the significant. Now is the time to overcome estrangement and heal old wounds.

To quote the mystic, John of the Cross,

> *"In the evening of life you shall be judged on love."*

In other words, the best way truly to overcome the fear of death, is to live life in such a loving way that its meaning cannot be taken away by death.

> *"The feelings of delight meant by heavenly joy and eternal happiness spring from nothing other than the love of what is true and good. The superiority of these feelings of delight to all those belonging to any love that exists in the world is completely unknown to those who suppose that all delight resides in worldly, bodily, and earthly things."*
> (Swedenborg. *Arcana Coelestia* section 10530)

17. Surviving a Catastrophe

Public Disaster

Many of us cannot understand why there is so much suffering in the world. A sudden and severe trauma that threatens death or serious injury can shatter our lives; like earthquakes, hurricanes and other natural catastrophes, transport disasters or violence by war combatants, criminals and terrorists. Psychologists have come to understand disasters much better in recent years. After experiencing a harrowing event, we can feel so overwhelmed that we start to think we are going mad or losing control over who we are. Our reactions may alternate between times of being empty of all emotion when we are numbed by shock and disbelief – just not being able to take in what has happened – and other times when we are extremely upset with intense re-living of the trauma as if it were happening all over again.

During the latter state, we may re-experience those feelings of fear, anger, helplessness, and horror that we previously felt during the disaster. Sometimes we think about what might have happened had we reacted differently. 'If only I had done this ... or that'. However, catastrophes usually happen suddenly and unexpectedly. The quickness of events gives us no time to prepare and takes us completely off guard. Unreasonable guilt feelings indicate that we are still trying to make sense of what, for most of us, is an extremely unusual happening.

As in bereavement, it is only natural for us to feel grief about something or someone important to us that is gone. Making sense of sudden loss and destruction can be very difficult. Perhaps the disaster badly damaged our limbs, destroyed our home, or even killed members of our family. Maybe it radically changed our lives so that we were obliged to give up an occupation or other rôles in life. In 2002 a forest fire made over 2,000 families homeless in one county in California. This was one of the worst natural disasters in the state. By 2006 many homes had been rebuilt. One couple, Jim and Maureen, moved into their replacement home with their teenage son after four years living in makeshift temporary accommodation. However, they were then faced with a higher adjustable-rate mortgage. On top of that, Jim was obliged to close his business, affected by the fire.

Selling their rebuilt home and downsizing became the preferred option but the housing market had changed. Buyers had become wary about living in fire-ravaged areas, even if the rebuilt homes included sprinklers, tile roofs and other protective measures, and so property prices dropped. Having failed to make loan repayments for several months and receiving no offers on the vacant property, listed for about half a million dollars, the couple not only expected repossession of their home by their mortgage lender with a cheap sale of their only asset, but also faced the prospect of bankruptcy.

All this just shows the fragility of the things of the world that we take for granted. Previously and without realising it, we had probably assumed that bodily and material things were permanent features of our lives. We thought they sustained us and that we could not do without them. However, having them badly damaged or lost, we realise how transient they really are – here today and gone tomorrow.

"Do not store up for yourselves treasures on earth, where moth and rust destroy, and where thieves break in and steal"
(Matthew 6:19)

"Even if (after death) you are attached to worldly goods left behind, you will not be able to possess them, and they will be of no use to you. Therefore, abandon weakness and attachment for them; cast them away wholly; renounce them from your heart"
(*Tibetan Book of the Dead*, ii,l. – Buddhist tradition)

One important thing we can do to survive emotionally is to realise that a sense of loss of material possessions and other negative responses are normal and will likely eventually pass in time, albeit in a gradual manner. We could make things a lot worse for ourselves by imagining that we are the only ones that the disaster has badly hurt.

Private Disaster

Although often extremely difficult to do, making sense of a catastrophe is key to dealing with it. For example, it is personally disastrous when those in power put us into prison with little hope of survival. In the depth of despair in the Auschwitz concentration camp during the second world war, Victor Frankl searched for ways to find meaning to his suffering and to the suffering of others. [1] He noticed some inmates wished to survive for the sake of others, for children or a spouse who awaited them; some, like him, for the sake of completing some unique life project; and some wished to survive to tell the world about the camps. Frankl states that, even when there is no chance of escape from suffering and death, there is meaning in demonstrating to others, to God, and to oneself, that one can suffer and die with dignity.

One day a personal disaster that affects few others, may ensnare us. It can be catastrophic only to oneself and one's immediate family to lose – or be about to lose – a well-paid job, an enduring state of physical health, or a life-long partner. Except perhaps for the bank manager or the doctor, other people may not even notice that any of these things have occurred. Whatever the scenario, when the blow falls, we can be just as shocked as if it were due to a natural disaster shared in common with our community. It is even worse as there will be no public recognition, sympathy and support for our individual plight.

Mohammed's family belonged to a minority religious sect. They had owned a jewellery shop in Iraq. At least they did before the invasion that toppled Saddam Hussein and the resulting state of anarchy and sectarian violence. Their shop was ransacked in the summer of 2004 and the family targeted. Mohammed believes the threat to them was because of their minority religion. This had been something preserved in the family for generations. Their beautiful daughter aged twenty was kidnapped and then murdered.

Such a personal catastrophe can cause a momentous upheaval to our lives – just as much as can a natural disaster. A personal calamity throws us upside down so that we feel in utter turmoil. Everything we thought we had worked for we may feel is destroyed. This could be anything we had assumed we needed to make us happy – in fact, things similar to those a public catastrophe could destroy; for instance physical fitness, good health, success in one's profession or business, a loving partner, cosy home, or being in a prestigious position with the material and social trappings that go with it. Our comfort zone is no longer available. The blow is harder to take if we had unwittingly assumed that whatever it was that we loved would always be there. We feel like shouting out 'It's not fair'. 'It's not the way things are supposed to be'.

Mohammed took his wife, mother and younger child and fled their home for Baghdad and then they managed to cross the border for the safety of another country. But exile in a neighbouring country meant living in a one-bedroom, dank basement that was all they could afford. They were not permitted officially to work and found, as in most of Iraq's neighbouring countries, that given their high number, Iraqi refugees were blamed for all kinds of social problems, e.g. increasing crime, unemployment and prices. Being members of a minority sect made it difficult for the family to know whom to trust – even amongst fellow displaced Iraqis. The plight of such people triggers our compassion and sorrow.

Like external ruin, a private disaster can happen unexpectedly – or at least that is how it seems at the time. Often, however, the signs would actually have been there long before the blow hit us. It was just that we did not see it coming. We had not noticed the warning indications - or rather, we did not want to notice. Perhaps issues left unattended within our sexual relationship led to a slow build up of tension. Perhaps our business was running at a loss and no longer tenable with contracts harder to find, but we had been in a state of unrealistic optimism, even though the end was staring us in the face. Perhaps recent events, for which we had not been able to find answers within our old convictions, constantly undermined our habitual ways of thinking about our life. Instead of re-examining our beliefs, we just shut our mind to what was going on. Now the beliefs seem to lie high and dry and discredited.

If we had ideals, we may not have very well thought out our personal philosophy or world view. What we did about it was probably more for the sake of making a gesture in favour of our principles rather than turning them into a vocation. There was much attachment to things of the world.

Positive Aspects

A life-changing event, whether due to public or private catastrophe, can shake us out of inner complacency. Take away the outward trappings and appearances of life, and the inner reality is laid threadbare. Before the disaster we may have been too busy to have worried too much about the meaning, worth or purpose of what we have been doing with a lot of our time. After a major disappointment or an emotional shock, we start to feel a stronger sense of dissatisfaction, and an elusive sense of lacking something. Life at times begins to feel empty, as those matters, which formerly absorbed so much attention, seem to lose some of their value. Our previous hopes have been dashed. Things or people in which we had put our trust have let us down – whether it be our worldly position, some addiction we turned to when feeling low, or someone we had depended on too much.

Despite throwing ourselves into external activity, the inner unease ferments and eventually breaks out as anxiety and even agitation. Roberto Assagioli designed psychosynthesis psychotherapy for people who are able and willing to work on personal issues in these terms. Individual clients vary as to how they react. Intellectual doubts and metaphysical problems sometimes appear to dominate; in others, the emotional depression or the moral crisis is the more pronounced feature. Many therapy clients begin to inquire into the origin and purpose of life; to ask what is the reason for so many things previously taken for granted. [2]

Life moves on following setbacks and so should we. When we are ready to get on with things instead of standing still in shock and bemoaning our loss, we will start to feel more alive. We experience a higher state as an illumination that makes things clearer and as a renewed energy for getting on with life. People report experiencing a wonderful release that does *not* soon pass. We realise that there is a lesson in what has happened. Had we seen the writing on the wall before the crisis overtook us we could have changed things sooner; however, better late than never.

We may have been immobilised by a change in our outward circumstances but gradually we may start to notice a small voice within us suggesting it is we ourselves who need to change. Perhaps we can find a new happiness – stop blaming others and fate for what has happened. Get on with it. Remember, when the going gets tough, the tough get going. We are never too old to move with the times, never so beyond it that we cannot adapt and find new things, new people, new relationships.

Doubts

The experience of catastrophe, whether personal or public, can drastically undermine our previously held beliefs about life. A big stumbling block for many is the doubt whether there can be a loving God in heaven given the extent of suffering taking place on earth. As I mentioned previously, we can conceptualise God as being like a loving parent who gives his child a certain amount of free rein. How else is the growing individual going to learn other than from making mistakes? We can then all have a sense of ourselves as free to carry responsibility for our own actions. The down side is the horrible consequence when humanity abuses its responsibilities. Needless loss of life and the traumas of terror and pain can take place because of human behaviour e.g. people unfairly distributing limited economic resources, unleashing destructive forces during warfare, or planning homes so cheaply that they collapse easily during earthquakes or flood because they are built without proper foundations or on flood plains.

I believe God, like a loving parent, permits us to make mistakes so we can learn the lessons of life.[3] He permits human folly that on occasion results in disaster. Human negligence, mismanagement, short-sightedness, greed, etc. are allowed – not because any innocent bystanders might suffer – but because, without permission for us to do what we want, we could not be free to follow or not our inner conscience. I might add that if God were to prevent all human suffering, there would be no spiritual challenge for us to meet the needs of others who are victims rather than attending only to self. This idea of God's permission of what is evil in the world, is very different from the mistaken idea, in my view, that misfortune is basically a punishment from God for human sin. I believe God punishes no-one. He does want us, however, to face the consequences of our actions. Unless we can freely choose what kind of people we want to be, we would only be automatons and not human.

Innocent Suffering

However, we cannot directly link all natural disaster with human behaviour. Sometimes, people do suffer not only through no fault of their own but also through no fault of others.

So, what are we to believe instead? That in a sort of vindictive way God, having a dark side, wants us to suffer? This view of God has been common in traditional Western religion. It is certainly how God apparently is portrayed in sacred scripture; a God of anger because of the rebellion of the people: so full of wrath that Christian theologians in the past have assumed that only a personal sacrifice by Christ could appease the Father's desire for vengeance. The psychologist Carl Jung was careful to distinguish between the reality of God and the God-image that an individual may have. As a psychological writer, he was reluctant to pronounce on the former. He accepted, as a God-image, whatever an individual claimed to experience as God, that which represented the person's highest value whether expressed consciously or unconsciously. Nevertheless, Jung himself did have a mixed view of God. His book *Answer to Job* expresses bitterness. This archetypal image is said to contain a light as well as a dark demonic side of the Creator. The traditional Christian teaching emphasised a dark side to God based on a literally-minded understanding of the Bible teaching that God's wrath was visited on 'sinners' and even 'non-sinners'.[4] Jung believed that illness, failure, humiliation, and tragic happenings that were inflicted on Job, were sent *not* by a loving Father God, but by a God who lets his dark son Satan have his way.

On the contrary, Swedenborg strongly affirms that God has no dark side for he is pure love and wisdom as shown in a life of healing and compassion seen in the reports of Jesus Christ.

In response to catastrophes and chaos, some of us may be inclined to give up altogether on the idea of God. However, such an attitude would mean a radical change in the way we view things around us. Instead of putting our faith in a spiritual source of our lives, we would be obliged to pin our hopes of happiness on the things of the world like a comfortable home, an attractive body, social status, and material comforts. Or we could look to human beings for our salvation, even though some of them have committed some unspeakable acts that make us cringe even to hear mention.

My own inclination is to think of innocent suffering as sometimes due to a fallen world of nature around us that not only mirrors the beauty of heaven but is also an echo of the ugliness of hell; not only the virtues of decency, honesty, kindness, but also the vices of depravity, deceit, and cruelty. We are familiar with a hellish state of mind that we sometimes see vividly portrayed in the theatre and on television. Like Swedenborg, I would maintain that God did not invent hell nor natural disaster. These instead reflect a state of heart and mind resulting from the way we human beings over many generations have corrupted what is good and pure. This negativity is created by us when we fall for the illusion that we can make ourselves happy through our own cleverness and self-seeking.

Enduring Reality

I would recommend we put our faith in things of divine spirit that no worldly loss can damage – things like consideration for others, pulling together, and trying to be positive in the face of adversity. A tragedy may bring it home to us that divine realities like compassion, belonging and courage, are the enduring bedrock of our lives and that the things of the world we previously valued so highly are mere illusions of happiness.

I believe heaven is the source of what is spiritually real. It inspires us on earth with a caring attitude, a sense of togetherness, an affinity with others. It also flows into us as a faith that makes us brave and full of hope. This is so because we each have a human soul, which can receive these heavenly feelings and thoughts. The Bible says that 'The kingdom of heaven is within you' (Luke 17:21); we are all capable of experiencing heaven in our daily lives. It is an inner state of mind; a spiritual reality that our bodily senses cannot detect. Nevertheless, it is a very real and permanent feature to human life that physical events cannot harm.

We can start to be more aware of the reality of heaven within ourselves and between others and ourselves. Then, gradually over a period we can adjust to catastrophic changes in our world. Our confidence can start to increase a little as we see heaven motivating the efforts of rescue workers in flooded areas; leading the deliberations of planners and politicians to be better prepared in places at risk, like, for example, setting up a world-wide Tsunami early warning system ; and giving those suffering loss, some comfort and financial expectation that they can recover their lives.

Even though we cannot see or touch heaven, becoming more conscious of this state of mind inspires us and fills us with hope. We cannot take the things of the world with us when we die; only things of the spirit. This shows that spiritual reality is more permanent and safe from destruction than what is merely physical; for a catastrophic event cannot destroy heaven. Rather, we find heaven interiorly within ourselves if only we would look for it.

"The final end in creation is an angelic heaven from the human race,"
(Swedenborg. *Divine Love and Wisdom* section 330)

18. Coming to Terms with Voices

Hearing Voices

A few of us hear voices not heard by those around us. It is at first disconcerting to hear others speaking inside one's head. Such voices sound like real voices, not the faint speech we usually hear as we think; but clear perceptions others cannot experience in the absence of external stimuli.

Outside of some medical circles it is recognised that to have so-called hallucinations does not mean the person is necessarily ill. For example to hear one's name called when there is no-one around is not uncommon. According to spiritualists a bereaved person may feel reassured when visited by a loved one who has recently died.

Many people who experience voices think of them as manifestations of an unseen presence. The following example[1] illustrates this although it is about a person who heard no actual voice. A college lecturer had gone to bed in his rooms at his college, when someone or something grasped his arm. This made him get up and search the room for an intruder without success. The next night after going to bed in the darkened room he lay awake for a while thinking about the previous night's experience, when suddenly he felt something come into the room and stay close to his bed. It remained only a minute or two. He did not see, hear, smell or have any ordinary sense of it, yet he said it caused him a horribly unpleasant 'sensation'. It stirred something more at the roots of his being than any ordinary perception. He was conscious of its going. Many may scoff at all this, saying it is just an active imagination at work. However, individuals have mentioned having these types of experience often enough to suggest they sometimes do occur.

We don't have to be mad to have these sorts of experience – although suffering from a severe emotional disorder may mean we are more likely to do so, particularly the negative experience of nasty accusative voices. The experience of hearing voices is often reported as distressing, threatening, or tormenting by those of us who may happen to have a severe psychiatric disorder. The voices may talk to us or about us. They may even be present all day and have the effect of preventing us from doing things in our daily life. They might insult us if we do not do what they want.

Although in this state we often encounter these voices as if they are coming from outside of us, the medical profession calls them 'hallucinations'; the assumption being that they do not exist outside our own mind. Yet, to the person experiencing the voice, it seems real enough and is *not* usually thought of as part of oneself. The hearing of voices can actually occur in some of us who are in healthy contact with reality and not suffering any mental disturbance. Nor do we have to take mind-altering drugs like LSD, or suffer from medical conditions like fever to experience them – although again these factors will likely increase the probability. Many so-called primitive peoples believe that almost every normal adult can go into a trance state and allow a god to possess them.

Joe Simpson, whilst climbing on the West Face of Siula Grande in the Peruvian Andes, fell from high up on the mountain and was left for dead. Frostbitten and slowly freezing to death he recovered consciousness to realise he had a broken leg throbbing with pain and unusable; he was precariously placed on a snowy ledge above a glacier and six miles from base camp.

'Cold had long since won its battle. I accepted that I was to die. Sleep beckoned insistently; a black hole calling me, pain-free, lost in time, like death'. Yet without help he amazingly survives to tell his story of extreme hardship.[2]

> *"It was as if there were two minds within me arguing the toss. The voice was clean and sharp and commanding. It was always right, and I listened to it when it spoke and acted on its decisions. The other mind rambled out a disconnected series of images, and memories and hopes, which I attended to in a day-dream state as I set about obeying the orders of the voice ".*
> (Simpson. *Touching the Void*)

He had to get to the glacier. He could then crawl on the glacier, but he did not think that far ahead. If his perspectives had sharpened, so too they had narrowed, until he thought only in terms of achieving predetermined aims and no further. Reaching the glacier was his aim. The voice told him exactly how to go about it, and he obeyed while his other mind jumped abstractly from one idea to another.

Some psychiatrically disturbed patients hear extremely unpleasant voices. Consequently, in the Western world, when healthy people are asked by journalists to give interviews regarding hearing unseen voices, they often fear ridicule. Unlike Joe, the rest of us tend to keep quiet about such unusual occurrences because we worry we may be thought to be mentally ill. Researchers have discovered that individuals only speak of extraordinary experiences when they are convinced they will not be treated as foolish or mentally unbalanced. They do then, readily and directly, answer questions put to them, and if they have no answers, they say so. Far from wishing to impose their own interpretations upon their experiences, they are often deeply puzzled by them and anxious for explanations.

Dreams

We hear voices of people speaking in our dreams. However, most of us forget all our dreams unless we happen to wake up around the phase of dreaming during the night. One can suspect it is because either we have deep restful sleep, not disturbed by dreams of a troubling nature, or more likely it is because it takes some close inward study to recall our dreams.

Attitudes towards the study of dreams have varied in the past. However, today people often think that dreams are a spontaneous and natural process presenting the central life concerns of an individual in a dramatic language. They appreciate that dreams seem to work by way of visual and auditory representation of inner thoughts. This has more power than ordinary speech. In a dream it is not only what the voices say, but also what happens and the visual scenes we observe, that can instruct us. Other people who appear in our dreams seem to reflect aspects of ourselves. The dream uses our memories and associations of ideas. It can be composed of individual associations or universal elements mixed or separately.

I am attracted to the view that some dreams can resemble mystical states. I am not talking about nightmares. Both types of altered states of consciousness are uplifting and raise our personal insights to a higher level; nevertheless, they are not conceptual but rather perceptual. The content of a dream appears to represent how we are in ourselves from a higher perspective. We sense, but do not comprehend, what is going on. Clinical psychologist Wilson Van Dusen suggests that dreams do not usually fit our ways of thinking and so we cannot easily understand and thus remember them.

It can be argued that personal study of our dreams has the potential to remind us of our needs, gives us another perspective on what we are doing, warns us when we are getting out of sorts with others, gives us an inside view of the value of significant things in our life, and clarifies our real values. We could study our dreams for they are one way in which we can be led towards the insights necessary for our spiritual growth.

Other Altered States of Consciousness

Since the rise of science and technology, society has tended to down-play the existence of the psychic nature of unusual phenomena like hearing voices. Yet, there is a range of common private experiences of sensing things not sensed by others, and where waking consciousness cannot account for what is going on. Like dreams, our other altered states of consciousness include images and sounds experienced on the edge of sleep, flash-backs of traumatic experiences as if they were happening over again, the heard voice of a recently deceased person, out-of-body experiences, and near-death experiences. These all appear to be extra-sensory.

Some of us have no conscious recollection of having had any so-called hypnogogic experience. This state occurs when we are drowsy between sleep and waking whether it is at night or in the morning. For others of us this may be a period of enchantment, with beautiful visions, sweet music and insights into ourselves. More common are seemingly isolated meaningless images, incomplete scenes, or bizarre or distorted images. It seems that the hypnogogic state symbolises whatever we happen to be thinking and feeling. Perhaps studying these fleeting experiences can possibly improve our awareness and make us more confident of beauty and wisdom in the natural depths of mind.

Causes

Swedenborg experienced dreams of an unusual nature where the dreamer keeps a degree of self-awareness as if awake. Today, psychologists call these lucid dreams. He also described visions of spirits and a spirit realm when the eyes were open. He is careful to distinguish this experience from ordinary imagination. Some people likewise report seeing apparitions.

Swedenborg's own extraordinary experiences started when he had been exploring the patterns of thoughts and images that arose in his mind during meditative and trance states. In his normal waking consciousness he learned to detect the process of what we term extra-sensory experience.

He discovered that the mind is naturally capable of becoming aware of symbolic images that reflect an inner awareness within the individual. Based on his extra-sensory experiences, he maintained that all of us have both internal and external sensation; with our internal senses we may at times be able to perceive a spiritual dimension to life which is normally hidden from view, and with our external senses we perceive the familiar physical universe of nature.

As referred to before, Swedenborg reports, from his extraordinary experiences, that the spirits of people in human form exist in a spiritual world. This realm, with its objects and scenes, is a projection, and a reflection, of the inner character – that is the spirit - of these people. An ugly environment represents people in a bad state and a beautiful environment people in a good state. He emphasised the reality to the senses of this non-physical existence. Moreover, he said that the voices he inwardly heard actually reflected the presence of those spirits who had bodily died but were alive in the spirit world. Some of these were of good and others of bad character.

Likewise, he said that some dreams come by way of spirits who are close to a person when he or she is asleep and who also have psycho-spiritual significance for the dreamer. Bad spirits bring on nightmares and deceptive dreams.

> *"With every individual there are good spirits and evil spirits. Through the good spirits, man has conjunction with heaven, and through the evil spirits with hell. ... These spirits have no knowledge at all that they are with a man, but when they are with him they believe that all things of his memory and thought are their own. Neither do they see the man, because nothing that is in our solar world falls within their vision."*
> (Swedenborg. *Heaven and Hell* section 292)

This may sound like a return to medieval myth. Swedenborg lived before the birth of psychoanalysis, since which, when anyone experiences dreams or hallucinatory material, psychologists tend to assume they must be pieces of the self welling up from the repressed unconscious rather than evidence of any hidden spiritual world.

However, the view of Van Dusen – who worked for many years with clients who experienced voices [3] – is in line with both depth psychology and Swedenborg's interpretation of his experiences. [4] I agree with Van Dusen's opinion, that the various states of extraordinary consciousness e.g. dreaming, the hypnogogic, trance states, voices, apparitions, lucid dreams etc. are different ways of viewing a single process, that is ordinarily unconscious. Such altered states of consciousness reveal a spiritual dimension of which the person is a part. This dimension also contains the inner world of mind with all its inner dispositions, tendencies, and values. The manifest world of spirit thus mirrors the inner psychological life of the individual. Waking consciousness in the physical body normally blocks out this inner psychic process, yet the world of spirit is experienced with the senses as just as real as the outer world of physical life.

Meaning of Voices and other Visions

People with severe mental illness may hear negative voices and, perhaps not surprisingly, this may tragically delay their personal development. If one develops delusions and loses rational thinking due to a sick condition of mind then one cannot reflect on and change direction – in a word one is no longer inwardly free to be able to reform life. However, there are other people who hear positive voices that do not disrupt their mental life and who can cope and regard them as a healthy part of their lives. The clearly rational Greek philosopher Socrates, for example, would go into a spontaneous trance consulting his guiding spirit, sometimes for hours on end. For a few of us, hearing actual voices inside us - rather than merely thoughts – and not heard by others, is of spiritual significance. We consider that the experiences give us a deeper understanding of the truth about life. Throughout history and even today, there are people like Joe Simpson who find some of the voices they hear to be inspirational and comforting.

When malicious voices are heard abusing and devaluing, it can be difficult to believe that others sometimes hear positive voices that give guidance and inspiration. One can better cope if one gets in touch with others who do have the positive experiences. I would also like to offer some hope to those afflicted in this way – believing as I do – that God who created and protects us is stronger than the voices from hell. I do not know when – before or after death – but I believe there will come a time under divine providence when all sufferers will once again be free of their affliction.

19. Shaking off Unhappy Moods

Feeling Fed Up

It is lovely to be full of the joys of spring. However, do we sometimes or perhaps often, feel fed up or in a bad mood? Nearly all of us know what it is like to feel down in the dumps. Sometimes we are stuck in an unhappy frame of mind. It is no fun feeling discontented and discouraged. The doctor may diagnose mild clinical depression even if our negative mood does not amount to feeling despair or having suicidal thoughts. All it might take for the doctor to make this diagnosis is for us to report that for a few weeks we have been feeling despondent, have been having difficulty finding pleasure and interest in things that normally attract us, and have been experiencing low levels of energy.

Unconscious Influences

What causes unhappy states of mind? External causes such as financial loss, bereavement or a redundancy may contribute to unhappiness. Alternatively, family or work stress may be the problem. However, people vary enormously in the way they respond to such events. Moreover, sometimes no obvious outward problem may be causing their troubles. Forces from within seem to be able to affect our feelings.

One of these is the way we think. We are all familiar with the idea that the pessimist's pot is half empty whereas the optimist's is half full. Likewise, it is typical of us human beings to assume that all unhappiness is externally caused. One might for instance have the idea that it is awful and catastrophic when things are not the way one would like them to be. It is expressed in such terms as "this is awful," "nothing could be worse," etc. Another example is when we say to ourselves "I can't stand it – It isn't possible to live with such frustration." Without realising it, such people unconsciously assume that they have little or no ability to control their moods because these are determined solely by events and circumstances beyond their power.

According to Jesus Christ, acting on spiritual ideas can free us from unhappiness and discontentment. As he said, "the truth will set you free" (John 8:32). True spiritual thinking, rather than mistaken ideas, about people and situations can change our negative feelings about them and about ourselves. He encouraged his followers to change their habitual ways of thinking and during his ministry in Judea he constantly challenged old ideas. One way of doing this was to teach in parables in which he provided alternative rôle models to the conventional ones, and thus encouraging his listeners to use their intelligence to think for themselves concerning the rational, moral and spiritual message.

One example is the story of the good Samaritan, who, despite being a member of a despised social grouping, actually showed more loving kindness than the respectable members of society. The way we think about our social responsibilities for meeting the needs of others who are worse off than ourselves can distract us from self-pity and the low mood that can accompany it. Another example is the story of the prodigal son who returned home, tail between his legs, yet received loving forgiveness, despite squandering his father's money. Unhappy feelings of defiance or resentment can change to contrition or forgiveness, as long as we challenge our ideas about what is the appropriate reaction to misdeeds and wrongdoing, both by ourselves and by others. The way we habitually think affects our moods in ways we do not often realise.

Normal Unconscious Influence of the Spiritual World.

The psychologist James Pratt believes that it is commonplace for us to experience what he calls mild mystic states. He says people have rarely described these vague experiences. The reason he gives is that those acquainted with them are frequently hesitant or ill-prepared to describe their experiences. They originate from a region of consciousness that he refers to as "the feeling background." [1] This sounds similar to Jung's notion of a collective unconscious (described previously in the chapter on being acceptable to others). In contrast to our sensory experiences, memories and ideas, Pratt claims, we are less aware of this 'feeling background'. It links us not only to our own personal pasts but also to our ancestors and to the race, in fact, in a sense, to all living things. It is thought to serve as the origin of life's values and also frequently constitutes that part of the individual that recognises value in others.

Through his unusual psychic experiences, Swedenborg discovered that unseen spirits are more important to all our lives than perhaps we might imagine. In other words, their rôle is not just as spirits of relatives and friends reported by those having a near death experience. They have more than the rôle of spirit guide contacting a medium, whose presence those with psychic gifts can also sometimes detect. Their rôle is not just to be the voices of spirits heard in altered states of consciousness.

Although this may sound incredible to the modern reader, Swedenborg wrote that spirits are also actually active in everyone's ordinary day-to-day life. This influence is said to be an unconscious one. The reason given is that each of us is a spirit and as such, we are all part of the 'spiritual world' although ordinarily we are completely unaware of this. It is only after the death of our physical bodies, when external sensation from the material universe no longer impinges on our consciousness, that the reality that we are each a spirit living in a spirit realm comes home to us.

Following Van Dusen [2], I take the view that experiencing bits of the unconscious self and perceiving what is represented in a world of spirit, are the same thing. Swedenborg says we unconsciously attract different spirits towards us according to our desires; the reason being a spiritual law - 'like attracts like'. Those with similar attitudes, dispositions, outlooks and values find it conducive and pleasant to be together.

We speak of being in low or high spirits. I fully accept this teaching that without our being aware of it, spirits linked with us conjure up images that both reflect and affect our state of mind. We only become conscious of this spiritual environment when we are in altered states of consciousness and more clearly when our physical senses die, although it has been there all the time. In this way, the spiritual world is a projection of its inhabitants living in a non-material (though still sensory) universal dimension, rather than having an existence limited to the individual. According to our natural tendencies and the character we are forming for ourselves - which are both central to our unconscious life - we unconsciously draw both good and/or bad spirits towards us. They inspire comfort and guidance but also may tempt us, or induce bad moods and delusory notions.

And so Swedenborg's position is that when alive on earth we are all ordinarily affected by both unseen positive and negative spiritual influences that raise or dampen our spirit. This dimension to life consists of spirits who, undetected by us, affect our thoughts and feelings. Neither they, nor we, are usually aware of this linkage and communication.

Furthermore, whether we attract to ourselves good or bad spirits depends on the attitudes we adopt. Good spirits are the channel for the good feelings and positive thoughts that pop into our heads. We sometimes experience these as creative impulses. Bad spirits pump into us selfish desires, fears, jealousies etc. particularly when we open ourselves to them and dwell on them. These are destructive impulses that connect with any unworthy tendencies within us. Like attracts like. The process is mutual and automatic until we cotton on to what is going on. We may never be conscious of the spirits to whom we are linked but we can be aware that the specific impulses that pop into our minds do not originate from within ourselves. Then we can choose to disown those feelings and thoughts that come to us that we recognise we no longer wish to entertain.

Limitations of Science

These are materialistic times when people tend to be sceptical about the supernatural or about anything existing that science cannot detect and measure. Yet it would be unscientific for scientists to pronounce upon anything beyond the scope of their measuring instruments, like for example the existence or non-existence of the human soul or of God. Similarly, biological science is not in a position to understand the subjective quality of human consciousness except by describing it in objective terms of chemical and electrical patterns in the brain. The realm of spirit, rather than the realm of matter, is a more likely candidate for causing non-material things such as consciousness with its elements of feelings and thoughts. Thus, many people do have an inkling that material things cannot explain everything and that there is something intangible and spiritual to life that they find hard to articulate.

John Lennon once said "Song writing is about getting the demon out of me. It is like being possessed. You try to go to sleep, but the song won't let you. So you have to get up and make it into something, and then you're allowed to sleep." Like him, many artists find themselves in association with some mysterious creative force that inspires or even drives their work. In addition, some scientists have reported having sudden inspiration; like Archimedes who jumped from his bath when he experienced a leap of understanding about the principle of displacement and Kekule who had a flash of insight regarding the ring structure of the benzene molecule when he was given a vision of a snake chasing its tail.

Our Inner Freedom

We might object that our inner feelings are authentic and define who we are, rather than coming from good or bad spirits. To some extent, this is probably true. Being human essentially is about the freedom to be what we want and become what we will. However, our freedom is not without limits. We are not free, for example, all of a sudden, directly to swap despondency for happiness, just as we have no power of ourselves to switch on creativity when composing music, or force ourselves immediately to feel affection for a particular person.

At the same time, importantly, we do have some freedom to be open to, or turn our backs on, different thoughts and feelings and thus, in effect, to receive or reject the influence of spirits who inspire various moods. As I have earlier said, I believe we are in a state of balance between good and bad inspiration. In so far as we have insight into our own inner motives, inclinations and ways of automatic thinking, we do have some freedom to choose with which to identify. Consequently we have some scope to link to different spirits and the moods they arouse. Sometimes however it might be difficult to move towards the change that we want to make. It may help to visualise this freedom in terms of turning the dial on a radio. We can listen in, either, on the one hand, to material that is uplifting and inspiring, or, on the other hand, to what is in tune with our sense of grievance, intolerance and other negative states.

Disowning Negative Influences

There is a Chinese proverb 'Honour the spirits, but keep your distance from them.' In other words, we do not have to permit the moods instilled by negative spirits to stay with us. After all, we think of tempting impulses - perhaps triggered by what we see on film or what we hear others say – as something apart from us, that we are not obliged to hang on to. In the same way, we do not have to identify with the depressive thoughts that come to us when these come out of the blue.

Thus, there is hope for those of us who wish to shake off our unhappy moods. We can start to recognise some of the negative thoughts that come to us, but which make us miserable. So when we are feeling captivated by a depressive mood, we can think of the thoughts and feelings associated with it as coming from something outside of ourselves. We can thus disown it. We can start to challenge thoughts about the world and the future that are unfairly negative. We can examine the illusions that deceptive spirits weave within us and start to question what they say about us. We may not be able to do anything well for example because of the thought "I'm useless". We can start instead to look for alternative ideas. Is it true that "Other people are interested in themselves and only talk to me out of duty"? Or that "Only bad things will happen in my life and I am helpless to stop them". We can question whether spirits are implanting falsehoods in our minds and whether such illusionary ideas are not our own. If they come from outside of us, we can choose to turn our backs on them and they no longer need have any power over us. We can stop identifying ourselves with the negative attitudes they represent. This is the way, more easily, to shake off our low spirits.

"The angels call forth the forms of good and truth residing with a person and set them opposite the evils and falsities activated by the evil spirits. As a result the person is in the middle and is not conscious of the evil or of the good; and being in the middle he is in freedom to turn towards one or towards the other."

(Swedenborg. *Arcana Coelestia* section 5992[3])

20. Reacting to Wrongdoers

Crime, Corruption and other Bad Behaviour

Mindless hooligans, dangerous drivers, and sexual offenders can get us very upset. In any society, a significant number of people do not accept they should follow the moral ideas of the majority; they do wrong because they do not see why they should not. On a less serious level, this includes the car driver who jumps the queue to park in the only space available and shrugs off any protest from those waiting their turn in an orderly way. Perhaps such a person thinks it is right to be selfish 'looking after number one'. On the other hand, many intentionally live a life of crime or immorality and, if they stop to think about it, know full well their behaviour is unjustifiable. Others do not stop to think about it and a few have such hatred and violence in their hearts they pose an enormous threat to the lives of others and the well-being of society.

After a dreadful crime has been reported, we can sometimes sympathise with the 'hang them and flog them' brigade even when we know the sentiment is mainly expressing our outrage and fury. We suspect a more civilised response would be better. Our strong emotion can tie in with a less than rational way of thinking and an unhelpful response that makes matters worse. The wrong heart, head and hands, so to speak. However, what is the appropriate way to respond to wrongdoing?

Alice, an elderly infirm woman, was a resident of a care home. She could hardly walk even with the aid of a frame. She needed full-time help to do even the basic things of life like managing her clothes, cooking and bathing. One day a care assistant called Debra entered Alice's room and removed several of her woollen jumpers from the wardrobe without a 'by your leave' saying they were "in no fit state to be kept any longer." Despite Alice's angry protests, Debra took away the clothes. The frustration of someone in such a dependent position, gave Alice the energy to slowly and painfully shuffle herself to the manager's office to complain.

A few days later Debra was seen hastily leaving Alice's room. Alice's suspicions were well founded, for she discovered a £10 note was missing from her drawer. In her younger days Alice had learned to write down the number of any bank note used to pay for goods in case of any dispute with shopkeepers regarding change. Fortunately, this habit had stuck and she took the piece of paper with the number to the manager. When accused, Debra unsuspectingly turned out her handbag only for the £10 note she had stolen to be identified as belonging to Alice. The money was returned, Debra dismissed from her job, and Alice no longer felt like a helpless victim.

In every country, it is against the law to steal. A society based on private property would collapse if no one respected this rule. However, I would point to the spiritual reasons for moral laws. By not taking from others, we learn respect for their needs. Regarding the biblical rule against adultery, as we resist the excitement of having an extra-marital affair, so we bolster trust and love for our married partner by valuing sex. Concerning the command not to bear false witness, we turn away from lies and deceit, so honesty and sincerity become part of our lives.

Another command is not to kill. Hate motivates murder. We can so hate someone that in a sense we could kill their good name by slandering their reputation. Yet, as we shrink back from spiteful malicious behaviour, so we can receive tolerance into our hearts. Military action is all about killing, but the alternative of pacifism may allow evil despots and vengeful politicians to destroy and enslave innocent people. In my view, the use of minimum force to bring about justice is often necessary. However, in the 'fog of war' this ideal may easily be lost. The individual soldier can only do what is right in his own situation. Where there is a questionably 'just war', his action may involve fighting, not for the sake of killing or conquering others, but simply to save his own life and that of his comrades.

External Restraint

Those in authority must restrain many offenders to some extent. This is for the protection of people and for keeping order in the community. No-one should be allowed to cause harm to another or get away with burglary, armed robbery, fraud, violence, etc. because we all need to live and work without fear in a fair and peaceful society. Having men of violence loose on our streets to create havoc and destruction, would not be sensible. Better that the courts place them in secure custody for all our protection. For other crimes the judges can sentence people, using forms of punishment other than imprisonment e.g. fines, community service orders, and curfews, although the public may suspect that these measures are ineffectively enforced. Some criminals may need a punishment of some sort simply to deter both them and others from repeating their offence and so that the justice system brings home to everyone what is unacceptable behaviour.

A sense of guilt and shame may be sufficient to prevent crime. It would be better if we all exercised self-restraint following the example of our rôle models rather than merely conforming to external restraint.[1] We would be taking on board the moral principles behind the law. My central assumption here is that our inner character is formed only according to what we freely choose to be.

Punishment

Many people believe that the threat of punishment sometimes deters burglars and fraudsters from repeating crime. This can be true to some extent and it certainly teaches the rest of us what is unacceptable behaviour. Nevertheless, psychologists studying punishment have found out that it is more effective for changing behaviour, when punishing animals or children, to combine punishment for undesirable actions with rewards for desirable actions. For instance, applied to those whom the police catch driving above the speed limit, this might mean attending a speed awareness course that involves learning about hazards and some practice driving around at the correct speed. The punishment for the offence is three penalty points but the system rewards drivers attending the course by letting them off these.

Taking such an approach with adults may not satisfy us when we wish to see someone suffer because of their crime. This is when we see a large part of punishment as retribution believing 'one gets what one deserves'. It is rather like revenge – a natural response but hardly a spiritual one.

Although many people who have committed criminal offences probably *need* punishment to deter crime and protect society from them, I would suggest that no person who does bad things ever actually deserves punishment *for its own sake*. This controversial idea is in line with a Swedenborgian concept of the divine. If God is the source of all mercy and compassion, how could he condemn anyone to suffer? I believe people often create and choose a criminal state for themselves, whereas God seeks the happiness of all, constantly seeking to raise people up out of their selfish states of mind. It is just that because some of us stubbornly cling to wrongdoing, that we need to learn the lessons of life the hard way, by being obliged to face the consequences of our actions. At the same time, we will all, at some point, be obliged to evaluate our own wrong-doing in the light of a true appreciation of what is good and true, honestly applied to our own behaviour and intentions.

Non-Judgmentalism

We cannot easily see what is bad in ourselves but seem to see it straightaway in others. It is easy enough to jump to conclusions about somebody. Yet this is not the recommended attitude.

> *"Stop judging by mere appearances, and make a right judgment."*
> (John 7:24)

Or as a Chinese proverb puts it:

> *"She doesn't look very bright, but you can't judge a book by its cover."*

It is possible and desirable to form a rational judgment discriminating between the rightness or wrongness of actions without at the same time judging the person's inner character. It is what juries in British criminal courts are supposed to do. This means judging and discriminating fairly rather than being judgmental or discriminative. We can say he or she has stolen and should not do so again but not say than he or she is bad. The same applies to ourselves. We can say 'I have done wrong but we should not say 'I am wicked'.

Why not? Well, if we think about it, we realise that there are people who do not seem to realise that stealing, adultery and lying are wrong. Mind you, others must have told them this at various times. However, knowing that teachers and society say something is wrong is different from understanding why it is wrong and acknowledging that one should not do it. It is different again from wanting in one's heart to turn away from wrongdoing. If a young person has grown up among adults who habitually steal, lie or are unfaithful to their partners, and think nothing of it, we can hardly expect them to realise that such behaviour is really bad, even if one is not caught. Or if told by parents, in a self-righteous, unrealistic or over-severe manner that certain things are wrong; in this circumstance the youngster will probably treat what the parents say with scepticism or hostility, and understandably so.

If we brand someone as evil, he or she may think themselves a hopeless case and give up trying to reform. If we speak in a judgmental way about others, they will almost certainly be hostile and in disliking us will probably reject any criticism of them that we make. I would say that it is much better to show tolerance and a clear belief that the individual is capable of improvement, whilst not denying or condoning any past wrongdoing. Only by genuinely repenting of our bad actions can we all hope to feel at one again with all that is good in life. Only by learning to forgive others can we hope to experience a sense of self-forgiveness.

> *"Those among them who are like angels …intend nothing but good towards their neighbour; and if they notice anything bad in someone they make allowances for it."*
> (Swedenborg. *Arcana Coelestia* section 6655)

21. Overcoming Obsessions

Introduction

The experience of having an intrusive thought is not uncommon. Unwanted thoughts and impulses plague us all at some times in our lives. When they are repetitive, unpleasant and difficult to resist, we feel obsessed by them. Then they may become troublesome and bad enough to interfere with the quality of our life. They may consist of simple thoughts in words such as "I might become ill". They may be mental pictures e.g. the image of something terrible happening. Alternatively, they can consist of urges to do a particular thing like harming oneself. The most common areas of concern in obsessions are sex, religion, dirt and violence.

Consequences

Because the thoughts are unpleasant or frightening, they make us feel very uncomfortable or anxious. We might try to reduce the obsessive worry by carrying out some action e.g. washing or checking, which we feel compelled to do. We might seek reassurance from someone, for example asking the doctor whether we are really ill. We may try to avoid the situations that trigger our anxiety; like, despite being in serious need of surgery, not going to hospitals where we might catch a disease. The places, people or things that we assume we must avoid can increasingly limit life.

Causes

Those of us who are temperamentally likely to become tense and anxious are more like to suffer from obsessive thoughts. If we are also over-scrupulous concerning small matters, then we are more likely to find distasteful or unacceptable thoughts difficult to shrug off. We find worries harder to control when we are distressed and they may become worse during significant times in our lives e.g. when we take on the extra responsibility of a new job, or when having children.

Our Unseen Spiritual Environment

Ordinary people have said they have felt an angelic presence in the face of death. Angels are thought to appear to little children. In addition, some people say that, on occasion, angels have helped them by comforting and healing them. [1]

As has been already described, the unseen spiritual environment around us inspires all our thoughts and feelings, although we are unaware of this.

I believe when we were young children, angelic spirits were linked with us implanting states of innocence, contentment and delight. As has been described previously, the idea is that this can often take place through the medium of loving parents. Although they are mostly unaware of the cause, and would find it very difficult to articulate it, people often look back at their childhood with nostalgia for such heavenly states of mind; for example, generally speaking, a sense of trust and lack of concern about time. This contrasts with the responsibilities of adulthood plagued by deadlines and worries. However, the childlike states of mind remain with a person who is free to draw upon them when reacting to whatever life throws at them. As has been mentioned in the chapter on loneliness, a sense of trust may have remained dormant for some time but it re-awakens if we turn our mind to what we think about, for example, the way God wants to provide for all of us.

We often speak about "when the spirit moves me" and about "getting into the spirit" of something. As adults, sometimes we notice our guiding light that inspires hope and confidence. At other times we are aware of a negative idea that gnaws away, unsettling us. The chapter on unhappiness described how we unconsciously attract either angelic or malevolent spirits towards us, depending on where we choose to focus our minds. The good news from Swedenborg is that unless we give ourselves up to what is unworthy, our guardian angels have the power to prevent horrible fantasies stirred by the lower kind of spirits.

As I have indicated, it is my view that we are subject daily to the thoughts and feelings coming from good and bad spirits. However, most of us are unaware of this unconscious inflow into our hearts and minds. We can observe this influence from beyond ourselves when we reflect on the impulses and fleeting thoughts that inspire or tempt us.

Obsessing Spirits

According to Swedenborg, after their bodily death, the earthly memories of individuals are gradually shut off and become inactive. In the next life, being aware only of the spiritual realm, one will gradually progress into inner thought and become less bound to what is external and worldly, such as the imagery of spatial objects. Yet, some spirits, particularly those newly raised from bodily death, still instinctively hunger for things on earth. Swedenborg wrote that intrusive thoughts could obsess our minds, coming from certain spirits when they are fixated on certain worldly things that have special associations for them. These spirits try to fasten our attention upon such things. They are not aware of us as being separate persons from themselves but believe that our thoughts are their own. This does not sound quite so fantastic if we can accept that the thoughts of our spirit are our own. When we are anxious or over-conscientious, we are liable to attract spirits who are the source of our obsessions.

Swedenborg also describes spirits known as 'the conscientious ones' who make meticulous enquiries into matters into which no such enquiries at all ought to be made and so burden the conscience. They are said to have no knowledge of what true conscience is because they make all issues into matters of conscience. If we are subject to their inflow of doubt and minute questioning about something, then ideas weighing us down are never absent.

"When such spirits are present they also bring a feeling of anxiety that registers in the part of the abdomen located immediately beneath the diaphragm... I have talked to them and have noticed that their thoughts do not extend to any concern for matters that have greater purpose or that are vitally important."
(Swedenborg. *Arcana Coelestia* section 5386)

Reducing Obsessions

Swedenborg records that in one of his struggles against certain spirits who were obsessing his mind, he finally found refuge by fixing his gaze on a piece of wood, and from this his thought was led to the wood of the cross, and then to the thought of God. By a shift of attention, he thus broke the hold of the evil spirits.

Another way of shifting attention, that is used widely these days in cognitive-behavioural psychotherapy, is the following straightforward technique. If we notice we are obsessively ruminating about something, we need to shout the word 'Stop'. If shouting out aloud is inappropriate because we are not alone, we can instead *imagine* that we are shouting the word. Immediately the train of obsessive thought is disrupted. For the technique to work we have to be able to believe that our thinking can both block or promote our ability to cope.

An appreciation and acknowledgment of what Swedenborg is saying adds power to this approach. If we are plagued with obsessive thoughts, we tend to assume that they have a compulsive power over us. This is understandable given their intrusive persistent nature. This assumption is also understandable if we assume that we are responsible for the obsessions. However, as has been stated earlier, when we realise we are subject also to rational and creative inspirations from angels, then we no longer attribute either the creative inspiration or the obsession to ourselves, but instead to sources outside of ourselves. The consequence of this important realisation is that we can be confident that it is possible to start to free ourselves from the hold of the infesting spirits as long as we do not identify ourselves with their desires and ideas. The thoughts they inspire need no longer obsess us.

22. Discovering Confidence

Introduction

It is very rare to find people full of confidence in all circumstances they encounter. In fact a lot of us do lack self-confidence in one situation or another. Some children naturally need more encouragement than others before having a go at something.

Success, however, in one area such as spelling or telling jokes can sometimes help in leading to self-confidence in other rôles. It is easy to see why. As someone does well in something, he or she forms an expectation of doing well in other things. The more things the person tries, then the more opportunities for success. Yet, for some of us, this growing self-confidence has not really happened. Perhaps our parents were too protective, inadvertently discouraging our moves towards self-reliance. If we held back from trying new things, we would *not* have experienced success and therefore had no opportunity to learn positive expectations of ourselves.

Some individuals are naturally self-conscious. We might go along to a party, not knowing anybody there, and not being at all sure that we will have a good time. Not finding it easy to talk to strangers or with people with whom we are not very familiar, we may become shy and awkward. Perhaps we are not confident when it comes to using our bodies in co-ordinated ways as when dancing or playing sport. Not being much good at these activities, we have consequently not practised them, and thus not developed confidence in doing them.

Improving Skills

Even when accomplished in one area it is still possible to have low confidence in another because we are actually not very good at a particular activity. Not everybody has skills in all things. We cannot all be persuasive salespeople, charismatic politicians, assertive business negotiators, brilliant dancers or whatever. When we assume we are helpless to change things, we unfortunately do nothing to improve our chances of doing well. However, even taking a small first step can help build our confidence because we are proving to ourselves that we can do something – that we are not powerless. We can help ourselves along the way by improving our skills as far as is possible. For example, we can improve our exam confidence by fine-tuning our study skills. We can improve our social and occupational confidence by dressing to look our best, especially if we have a tendency to look a bit on the scruffy side. We are going to get more respectful attention from others if we have polished shoes and pressed clothes.

Negative Expectations

Nothing breeds confidence as much as success. Anyone can get into a downward spiral of low self-confidence, negative thinking, and poor performance at some challenging task resulting in further negativity. The way to tackle this kind of pattern, of course, is to be honest with ourselves about how we are our own worst enemies. Is it so likely that we will do badly at something? What is the evidence that our assumptions are correct? Often they are not; for example believing that we could not possibly find someone at a party with whom to get chatting. When having to compete for a job, we are not likely to win if we keep imagining someone else would do it so much better.

'If at first you don't succeed – give up' is an unhelpful motto! No wonder some of us wonder why we never experience any fun. After all, it is often unrealistic to expect to do well the first time we try something new. It is much more likely that we will have a few setbacks on the way before we can start to master a new skill – whether this is a practical or social skill.

Fear of Failure

Janet, in her mid-twenties, had been an office worker for several years. She was the sort of person who played it safe in life. During her childhood, her parents, in trying to set high standards, had unwittingly emphasised any mistakes she might have made, whilst doing things at home. By the time she was an adult, she had come to feel reluctant to try something new. She would feel mortified if she were to fail. When her manager asked her to take on a new rôle on a temporary basis whilst his personal assistant was away, she was quick to make up excuses why she would not be able to do this. Throughout her life, she had avoided challenges not expecting to do well at them. No wonder she had poor confidence, never giving herself the chance to experience success. If only she had taken on the rôle, she might have found that organising someone's diary, making arrangements over the phone, and accompanying the boss to business meetings, might not only have proved enjoyable for her, but she may have received some positive feedback for her efforts. Her frame of mind might have switched from concern over doing badly to looking forward to doing well.

Some of us make failure a catastrophe. Like Janet, we assume that not to do well at something would be the end of the world. We did not make any friends in our new job to start with – so what? Give it time. Our attempts to learn a musical instrument resulted in our family groaning during our music practice – so what? Practice when no-one is listening. We failed to make a date with the person we liked – so what? Try again another day. Janet's mother felt like sticking a placard on her daughter's bedroom wall. 'Nothing ventured, nothing gained'.

Self-Pity

Sometimes, perhaps without realising it, when we have very low self-confidence, this is because we do not actually *want* to succeed at anything. This may sound incredible but some of us would rather fail and then enjoy the pleasure of self-pity and sympathy from others. The more we fail, of course, the less confidence we will have. The more self-pity we indulge in, then the more do we become less motivated to try something; self-doubt growing deep down within us. Other people will only give us so much attention and time to try to build us up and encourage us, and then they are going to give up if they see we are not making any effort. With a continuing sense of self-doubt, we also come to depend on what others think about our personal choices and about what we do.

Over-Confidence

The confident person may discover that he or she is not as confident as once thought. What was posing as confidence was actually a false sense of over-confidence. Sometimes politicians believe the half-truths of the party-line that they voice and they end up accepting as true their own propaganda! As a result, they end up being put under pressure by journalists and others to defend the indefensible. Likewise, the rest of us are quite capable of believing the excuses we offer up to justify our mistakes and failings. In other words, we can get out of touch with how things really are. We can fail to distinguish between our private thoughts and how we come over to others. We can deceive ourselves just as we can deceive others regarding our real attitude. For what we do may not be due to confidence in our choices but rather to concern about how others might see us. How we think of ourselves may not be due to confidence in our own ideas, but rather to how others might criticise them. Saying and doing things for the sake of respect and reputation is a sign of fear rather than confidence.

Thrown by Calamity

Learning an occupation, sharing life within a sexual partnership, starting a family and home and building up financial security etc. caught us up as young adults into a whirlwind of activity and excitement. What we were planning may have developed well; our career, family and other relationships progressing satisfyingly. Some of us may even feel some self-confidence when now we evaluate ourselves in terms of our occupational or academic reputation, the extent we are in a position to exercise financial power, or the trappings of modern life we have acquired.

The trouble is the future is uncertain and things sometimes have a habit of going pear-shaped just as we have started to get a bit complacent about life. There we were, outwardly doing well, when a time comes when something appears to hinder our path. The close friend with whom we spend a lot of time announces his or her decision to emigrate, the boss turns round one day saying the company we work for has gone bust, or the doctor suddenly announces those minor ailments we were having are signs of a progressively deteriorating serious illness. There may be a crisis of doubt. Whatever the reason, life shakes our self-confidence and we no longer trust in our own abilities to save the day. In adjusting to these calamities we may experience times of frustration and worry; feeling vague anxiety, estrangement from the people around us and a sense of aimlessness. Our trust in the future is undermined. Any over-confidence and conceit in our self-intelligence we may have had lets us down and we become discouraged. No wonder they say 'Pride comes before a fall'.

Questioning our Values

Calamities may bring us up short. However, they do oblige us to reconsider the bigger picture. We find ourselves contemplating our lot and reflecting on the life we lead and the society we are living in. Then we are perhaps more likely to start to notice some contradictions around us; such as the beauty of nature and the ugliness of mankind's world of industry; the innocence of infancy and animals compared with the scheming deceit sometimes found in human commerce and politics. Another example for some of us is the trust shown by our children, compared with the distrust we sometimes feel for our colleagues and neighbours. Thinking about such matters, we realise we have tended to take for granted some of the givens of our world without deeper questioning. As we grew into adulthood, we had little time to ask the hard questions about life, the cosmos and death, that we may have asked as children, and so we forgot them.

So far in this chapter, I have talked about placing confidence in learning new capabilities, in examining and developing realistic, rather than unrealistic negative assumptions, and in facing fears of failure, all in relation to specific situations. However, we may wonder if these things are enough to reassure a growing general unease with life as a whole.

We would be mistaken to put our confidence in quick fix solutions, the – here today and gone tomorrow – sentiments of celebrities, and whatever is the current fashionable social attitude, if it lacks any careful analysis, any exposure to critical comment, or any deeper thought about its implications.

The 'Whole of Being'

So when it comes down to it, in what can we place our confidence? In our own abilities? In the ideas of others? Or in something beyond all of us? One example of the last of these three possibilities is to do with what the secular psychologist Abraham Maslow called 'the whole of Being'. He had studied exceptional people. The ideal values of what he termed 'Being' that he found in these individuals included justice, beauty and truth. [1] We may remember the final movement of Beethoven's ninth symphony – said by many to be one of the most triumphant and joyful movements in all music. Yet, the composer wrote it at a time when he was suffering disappointment in love. At one level, his life was a negative experience with everything around him seeming to overpower him. The music, however, shows us his intense inner life that could be both joyful and at peace, despite the adversity of his outer world. Within was an ideal view of life that he carried within himself, but which the world could not meet.

Maslow labelled thoughts concerning such ideals as 'B cognition' (B for Being) that he distinguished from 'D cognition' (D for deficiency). This ties in with his distinction, mentioned previously, between growth and deficiency motivation. An example of a growth motive being an interest in finding meaning in adversity and an example of a deficiency motive being a need for comfort when hungry, cold and wet. It is suggested that the more we can understand what has been called 'the whole of Being', then the more we would be able to tolerate what appears at first glance to be inconsistencies and contradictions in the way we think. Apparent opposites can disappear. For example the apparently opposite concepts of sickness and health may fuse and blur when we use 'B cognition' when, instead, the symptom is seen as a pressure towards health, or when neurotic avoidance is seen as the best way of dealing with a troubling situation, given the person's limited range of coping skills. Maslow writes about many similar apparent dichotomies that disappear.

I would suggest that a genuine rational understanding involves spiritual ideas. These illuminate the truth behind apparent dichotomies and contradictions in life that B cognition also resolves. Another example is the spiritual principle of conjugial love focused on in earlier chapters, that illuminates the seeming dichotomy of sexual desire and romantic attachment, for these are no longer opposite when both are present in the same relationship.

Religious people might say that 'B' thoughts in line with the 'whole of Being' are on a higher level than 'D' thoughts associated with the gratification or frustration of our natural needs, like those to do with bodily comfort. I am sure that what really provides confidence is not so much what we do in meeting our natural desire for comfort and status, but rather our activity to do with deeply held ideals and values associated with B thinking. A car mechanic will feel confidence in his work if he values providing a quality service, thinking about how to do his best in a sincere, reliable and considerate manner. A shop keeper will feel confidence in his rôle if he values honest trading; not ripping off customers by selling out-of-date food or damaged goods, but rather thinking about giving them sufficient time to see what things are actually spot-on for their requirements. The confidence is in the value of the ethical principles that sustain our efforts.

Our Small Part to Play

Trying to see how we fit into the organisation in which we work, or the social network in which we have a role, can also help our confidence. If we think we are needed, we feel we have a rightful place because of our special individual contribution. Another way of seeing the 'whole of Being' is to think of Swedenborg's concept of the 'Universal Human'. This is the ideal of all people arranged in a functional relationship corresponding to the organisation of the enormous number of constituent parts of the human body.[2] Similarly, in common parlance, we speak of a public or private body like a government agency or a commercial company that can be thought of in terms of a head, (the chief-executive), a mouth (the public relations officer), and an arm (the specialist staff) and so on.

"Just as each of us has one body with many members, and these members do not all have the same function, so in Christ we who are many form one body, and each member belongs to all the others."
(Romans 12:4)

In other words, we each have unique contributions to make. For we each have a different part to play in the grand scheme of things. The muscles operating in the body in pairs are antagonistic and this allows control of our limbs. Otherwise:

"If all pulled in one direction, the world would keel over"
(Yiddish proverb)

In diversity comes completeness. I would say God has individually created each of us to fit into the greater whole – the divine design of the whole of humanity as one community. Consequently, all of us can have confidence in our planned individual importance. God continually shapes us with developing abilities to enable us – if we so wish – to take our place in the perfection of the whole.

Faith in the Divine

The religious traditions make a distinction between outer and inner thinking, that is to say, between perception of the senses and spiritual perception. The worldly-oriented person, who only relies on what the senses tell him or her about life, may have difficulty appreciating – let alone trusting in a spiritual perspective.

"He who has understanding, whose mind is constantly held firm – his senses are under control, like the good horses of a chariot driver."
(Katha *Upanishad*, iii, 6 – Hindu tradition)

"Religion tends always towards the subjection of the senses, …because it desires to make the spiritual man dominant, in order that the truly rational man may govern the man of (the senses)."
(Eckartshausen. *The Cloud upon the Sanctury*, i. - Roman Catholic mysticism)

"…the Spirit of truth. The world cannot accept him, because it neither sees him nor knows him. But you know him, for he lives with you and will be in you"
(John 14:17)

Instead of relying on worldly things, we can put our confidence in the power of the spirit of love and wisdom. This is the clear view that enlightens our way forward. Our real strength and ability to face the world comes from God working in us rather than in self-confidence, as such, because we have confidence in the divine love within.

"No spiritual confidence exists if it does not flow in by way of the good of love and charity"
(Swedenborg. *Arcana Coelestia* Section 4352)

23. Living through Crisis

Introduction

John is a fifty year old man, who sought help for states of anxiety and depression. He could not fathom what was wrong. He had always been a confident person. He was married and their children had grown up and were now living away from home. The couple had altered their house and garden and now had their home as they wanted it. The neighbours and locality had become familiar and a part of him felt comfortable living where he was. He had a settled job in a successful company where he was a middle manager. However, in talking to a personal counsellor he found himself voicing self-doubts and uncertainty about where he was going in life; questioning his lifestyle, his career and even his marriage. He felt he had been drifting along, no longer with any sense of direction. He had lost touch with the ambitions that he had once had, but vaguely felt he had not accomplished what he wanted to do. He wondered if he wanted to get his youthfulness back.

New Spirit of Truth

This is a time of inner crisis for John. Perhaps life had become a little less hectic with fewer hurdles to jump all at once. It now seems as though there is more opportunity for him to hear his inner self telling him things he does not want to hear; like the need to let go of the old and do things differently. But he does not know what this means in practice.

How will those of us who have a similar experience respond? By going into denial about our own part played in the difficulty? By projecting blame on to others? Or perhaps by starting to learn a new humility and accepting in our hearts that we need help.

If we pay attention, a new spirit of truth can shine on our inner life.[1] It is as though we are being exposed to our own complacency. We may start to notice an attitude of smugness and self-satisfaction that previously lay hidden. We may then realise the huge discrepancy between how we had been seeing ourselves as compared to our real self. We start to appreciate the mixed motives behind so much of what we do. This exposure can be terrifying and painful. No wonder John felt anxious and depressed. Many of the things we have done have stemmed from a self-centred orientation, whilst in our own eyes we were acting in a worthwhile way. We can begin to grasp the extent to which we were living in a fool's paradise: how much we were kidding ourselves concerning what was worthwhile in us. If we resolve to change, it is usually after we have taken an honest appraisal of the situation.

In John's case, he came to realise that being pre-occupied with paying the mortgage, keeping senior managers happy and cutting the lawn at home, plus all the other work he had done on the house, was not really what life is truly about. He was able to laugh at his past mistakes and folly. Laughing at ourselves is a great alternative to self-condemnation.

The individual may then enter into an exalted state that dispels former doubts, solutions to problems may well become apparent, and a new sense of security be experienced. Trying new ways means taking control rather than simply letting things happen to us or responding to situations with knee-jerk reactions. For John this meant doing things for others rather than only for himself. One thing he saw was a need to get involved with his local school, acting as an unpaid governor – in other words, trying to put something back for what he had taken from the local community.

Reawakened Self

Such an exalted state does not go on for long. A profound change to our personal self requires more than just new inspiration. Facing new challenges is not easy. John had to force himself to go out on wet cold evenings to school meetings. When we do try to do things differently, it does seem that progress can be two steps forward and one step back. For our habitual pattern of being will re-assert itself, although not quite in the same way. A sense of deeper values becomes active in our mind and we start to criticise ourselves for falling short of the new hopes and expectations. So much so that we tend to make the mistake of assuming we have fallen down and are in a worse state than before the crisis had developed. New inner tensions then arise as we start to recognise which of our old ways we should be giving up to meet the new ideals. This is the price we pay for the newly awakened conscience.

It has been pointed out by Roberto Assagioli [2] that during this eventful period one experiences life as full of changes, of alternations between light and darkness, between joy and suffering. It is a long and many-sided process of development. It includes phases of active removal of obstacles to the inflow and operation of super-conscious energies. These are phases in which the person must let the higher self work, enduring the pressure and the inevitable pain of the process.

Self-Intelligence and Self-Merit

The religious attitude is to look to God as the inner source of all that is good and true in life.

"He guides the humble in what is right and teaches them his way."
(Psalm 25:9)

"The man who is united with the divine, and knows the truth, thinks, 'I do nothing at all.'"
(*Bhagavad Gita* 5:8 – Hindu tradition)

However, even then, without realising it, we tend to keep forgetting where our good ideas come from, and continue in life as though they originate in ourselves. We ascribe what we think and achieve to our own good sense.

The outward appearance of everything we encounter tends to seduce us. The danger into which we sometimes fall is to rely on the illusions of self-intelligence and short-sighted reasoning, for example, to believe that only what science can research actually exists. This self-satisfying attitude to our own ideas and rôles can even sometimes come across as vanity or conceit, but more often, it hides itself from view. Inside we subtly enhance our self-image and elevate ourselves to the moral high ground where we place a self-righteous emphasis on the outward appearance of being good and right in what we say and do. This can show as an inflexible adherence to doing things in the same old way as a sort of ritualistic habit. It can also show in our smug insistence on having the right beliefs when this is at the cost of both selflessness and free growth, of the spirit of generosity.

We think of our importance within our organisation or social group. So, like the John who had counselling, we might say "No matter what the current economic climate, I'm too astute and knowledgeable a business person to go under." Or "No matter what my weakness for sexual excitement might be, I'm too good and worthy a provider and family carer to be rejected by my partner."

As children, we may have been innocently pleased with ourselves when we earned that gold-star for good behaviour. As young adults, we may have felt pride in our academic accomplishments. Feelings of self-merit were stepping stones, helping us along the way towards personal and occupational standards towards which we were aspiring. However, although we reached a point where external rewards no longer spurred us on, we carried on praising ourselves.

The lesson of life can be sharp. As mature adults, we learn about how we have been seeking self-merit by attributing the good we do to our own goodness rather than originating from a higher spiritual source.

Taken to extremes, the state of mind that wants to take away from God the credit for what is good and wise in human living, is the condition of do-gooders looking down self-righteously on others. It is looking to the respectable side of our life for such things as a good name, prestige and success. These considerations might well be motivating the good things we do.

Without realising it, we may even engage in a self-centred manipulation of others and situations, all in the name of what we are claiming to be right and helpful.

One example of this is when the religious person manipulates knowledge of religious teachings or church position for the sake of control over others and the good opinion of others. Such an individual may do these things, in the name of doing what people regard as what is good, when in reality they are trying to impose dogmas and creeds, forms of conduct, and, in effect, making threats and promises by arousing people's fears.

Renewed Hope

When we honestly appraise ourselves for what we are deep down, we need no longer make up excuses.

> *"Count your rectitude as foolishness, know your cleverness to be stupidity"*
> (*Lao Tse Tao Teb King*, xiv. Taoist tradition)

This is being genuine with others instead of constantly trying to hide our true selves from them. Only by an authentic relationship with others, our God and ourselves can we hope to stop deceiving ourselves and find a hopeful way forward.

Those of us with a deep faith in God are never likely to lose hope, whatever, in life, threatens us. The spirit of truth and love lives on. However, such faith does lead to consequences. For there can be no new birth without some pain – there is no letting go of former things without some pain of loss.

> *"I tell you the truth, no one can see the kingdom of God unless he is born again."*
> (John 3:3)

This personal change is all to do with a new sense of ourselves, a realisation that, although we matter, the universe does not revolve around us, a forgetfulness of self-interest, a sense of being a small, though valuable, part of our social and physical world where we belong, and a dropping away of any anxiety that afflicted us during our personal crisis.

> *"The divine state of peace which exists inmostly ... manifests itself in external things through the removal of evil desires and false ideas; for it is these that cause all unrest."*
> (Swedenborg. *Arcana Coelestia* section 3696)

24. Receiving Hope through Despair

The Pit of Despair

Occasionally some of us find ourselves in a pit of despair when any possibility that things will improve seems lost. No longer taking any pleasure in life, and feeling totally drained, we hardly care what happens to us or to other people and feel we can no longer concentrate on any tasks or take any decisions. If we see ourselves as bad or worthless, we may want someone to punish us and may even see death as the only escape from the emotional pain of living. Suicidal impulses may come to us especially if a persistent, pessimistic outlook dominates and life seems nothing but a hellish nightmare.

Nevertheless, we are wrong in our belief that suicide is a solution. When we think that we are trapped and hopeless, our thinking is illogical, distorted and skewed. Somehow, we realise that this may be the view of other people, for often we are concerned that others would criticise us if we were to tell them of any thoughts of suicide. Talking about such things with someone in whom we can trust, or using crisis telephone support may bring some relief. Trying to defeat a severe level of depression without also gaining professional help is unrealistic, especially if we were considering putting thoughts of self-harm into action. Of potential value are medication, emotional support and talking therapy. One thing these give is the realisation that a profoundly negative mood will not go on forever.

Illusion of Meaninglessness

Sometimes there is a spiritual dimension to our depression. Shakespeare's Macbeth wanted power and status. Yet he said:

> *"Life is but a walking shadow... a tale told by an idiot,*
> *full of sound and fury – signifying nothing."*

We may also notice the pointlessness of our worldly desires as ends in themselves.

The failing to do with one's life all that one knows one can do, appears in the writings of existential theorists. This kind of inner despair is in line with Swedenborg's thought concerning not having a meaningful and useful life shared with others. Specifically this can arise when we feel apart from people and no longer belonging to a family or community. We fear harming our relationship with those people in our lives who mean something to us, such as lover or child. There also may be a fear of losing belief in, and inspiration from, spiritual principles that have uplifted our lives. These ideals now seem threatened by our desire to go against them in terms of, for example, self-indulgence or sexual fantasy.

Illusion of Alienation

To fall away from society and into what is unfamiliar and unknown can be extremely disorienting and disagreeable. One feels different, separated from normal ways of thinking and doing things, and unsure of the way forward. It is being vulnerable to emotional distress, tiredness, and very low mood. Alternatively, we may indulge in various kinds of addictions, escapism or risk-taking behaviour, expecting them to reduce the pain of dislocation and loss. Whatever appears on the surface of our awareness, there is an underlying anguish because of an inner sense of alienation.

Certain triggers for alienation have grown in recent times, because of our automated life and bureaucratic society and of the widespread materialist sense of values. Existential thinkers have put into words this state of estrangement from any truly human sense of reality and community. If we deny ethical and spiritual values, there is a great danger of our failing to have any reverence for, or sensitivity to, the world of nature, or any real contact with anybody in our social world.

Illusion of Condemnation

Some of us who are severely depressed may feel a despairing sense of unworthiness and guilt. Let us realise that darker forces within the mind encourage our self-condemnation and that we can gain some control over these. Just as we can receive creative inspiration from a higher source, so we are capable of receiving destructive impulses. These negative thoughts can have no power over us as long as we do not identify with them as our own. As I have pointed out, Swedenborg's visions of the spiritual realm convinced him that there are those he called 'evil spirits' as well as good angelic spirits, who unconsciously influence us. The evil ones desire nothing more than to pop into our minds self-damaging thoughts.

We are at risk of losing hope when they foster in us the illusion that we will suffer a future of punishment and torment. Yet, Swedenborg testifies to the unconscious presence with us also of angelic spirits who illuminate in us what we have known to be right, defending us against irrational illusions. He wrote that angels have the power of restraining evil spirits, defending us against their malicious influence. Therefore, through angelic help, we retain some freedom of thought to challenge our negative expectations.

Despair as Spiritual Testing

Prior to our periods of deep depression we may have experienced something of a fulfilling creative life, then feel deeply sad at losing touch with the mysterious joy associated with this. In a similar way, feelings of despondency or worse can be experienced by those of us undergoing the up-and-down process of spiritual growth, when we lose hope in the spirit of love and faith.

> *"I am bowed down and brought very low;*
> *all day long I go about mourning...*
> *I am feeble and utterly crushed;*
> *I groan in anguish of heart."*
> (Psalm 38:6-8)

Christ went through this experience of lost hope, and his inner anguish on the cross is shown by his crying out "My God, why have you forsaken me".

Yet, hope springs eternal, for this despair, if part of a state of spiritual testing, I believe, is a temporary phase we go through, for the sake of our developing faith. For example, Swedenborg says that those, who are being changed, are brought into a state of no longer knowing what is true. Understandably enough, this results in a state of grief over what is lost. It is part of a process that he calls 'vastation'. This is a humbling process. We cannot expect the individual to receive inner illumination from God when false notions are in the way. Mistaken ideas to which the person is persuaded hinder divine enlightenment because they derive from self-intelligence. Until one loses one's own ideas, one cannot receive the new light. [1] However, no longer to remember or understand the way we thought about important matters would bring unhappiness to anyone.

Salvation from Despair

When we are suffering states of spiritual temptation, it appears as if God were absent, (although in truth, Swedenborg insists, God is closely present). The illusion is necessary in order to oblige us to battle against what is unhealthy and bad still sticking to us. This temporary condition of dejection helps us realise the need to call upon God to save us and for us to acknowledge that we can only hope to conquer the lower forces of the mind by his power and not our own. Only through a broken and contrite heart can we learn to turn to God for salvation from despair, rather than rely on the illusion of self-sufficiency. [2]

Temptation states are part of a continuing cycle of individual consciousness. I have noticed from my own experience, regardless of whether I have yielded to tempting thoughts and desires, I afterwards experienced a period of relative inner peace. God rules everything, but he takes the long view, and this is very different from our own concerns that anchor us to this place and time. I believe he permits nothing bad to take place, such as personal despair, unless something worse would otherwise have happened – worse in the sense of being detrimental to our destiny, such as too smooth an experience of life that breeds only complacency.

When such negative desires grow within us, we may begin to mourn the loss of what is positive. However, in putting the negative to one side we grow in freedom to find our higher self. As we gain a sense of fulfilment in a new useful rôle for the benefit of family and community, we will have started to prevent pleasure-seeking and self-serving activities from ruling our heart. Only then can we hope to find new values and an enlightened meaning to our existence. However, this process of change may involve states of emptiness before a more spiritual life has the chance to gain ground within us.

When we struggle against the forces of darkness, a state of hope will replace our state of despair: hope of belonging to a community of people with whose values and goals we can identify: hope of finding a sense of purpose through the setbacks and confusions of life: hope of sensing a spirit of forgiveness; an acceptance by others of ourselves and self-acceptance, despite the many mistakes we have unfortunately made. And if we are deeply Christian in our religion, there is a forgiveness in the sense of experiencing the loving compassion of our Lord Jesus Christ, the loving shepherd who wants us all back into his protective fold.

"They may receive the perception of good and truth, which perception they are not able to receive until those false persuasions originating in what is their own are so to speak softened. And it is the state of distress and grief even to the point of despair that effects this change. What good is, and indeed what blessedness and happiness are, nobody with even the sharpest mind is able to perceive unless he has experienced the state of being deprived of good, blessedness, and happiness. It is from this experience that he acquires a sphere of perception; and he acquires it to the same degree that he has experienced the contrary state."

(Swedenborg. *Arcana Coelestia* Section 2694[2])

25. Drawing Ideas Together

Holism

I have found the books by Swedenborg to be rich with illuminating thoughts that are highly relevant to us in so many ways. I hope that some of his ideas presented here have led the reader to form a similar conclusion.

Together his teachings give a holistic theory. By this, I mean his system of thought tackles the heart, head and hands of daily living. [1]

Our heart is to do with what we feel and want – our affective side. Our head is associated with what we know and think – our cognitive aspect. Our hands represent what we do and say – our behaviour. If hands saying things sounds a bit strange, then remember that sometimes actions speak louder than words!

As Dante says:

"The principal powers of the soul are three – to live, to feel and to reason"
(*The Banquet*, iii, 2)

Swedenborg's ideas are in line with these psychological concepts of affective, cognitive and behavioural function. The three-fold terminology, that permeates all of his writings, reflects this. He writes about good or bad desires of the will, true or false ideas of the understanding and useful or disorderly actions of the body. The feeling, thinking and doing of daily living.

Consider these three aspects of troubled people. They are all likely to be negative. One may feel a loser and a failure, having a poor opinion of oneself and as a result give up easily on tasks and challenges. Or one may feel unloved and lonely, believing others are untrustworthy or critical and as a result avoid people. Or one may get frustrated and angry with oneself, believing that there is no way forward and as a result harm oneself. In other words, having negative feelings of the heart ties in with negative thoughts in the head and self-defeating behaviours of the hands.

Psychotherapists cannot facilitate change in all three aspects of a person all at once. One, however, has to start somewhere. Actually, the psychodynamic therapies start with the feelings, the cognitive therapies with the thoughts, and the behavioural therapies with behaviour. All schools of therapy aim eventually at the linking of all three together. This is because concern is for the wholeness of the individual and a realisation that only when there is congruence between, or integration of, the various sides to an individual can well-being and inner development be achieved.

Ideally, these three should be positive and link together in harmony if we are to thrive and experience well-being. Then in our heart we would have good rather than bad intentions, and an interest in, rather than an aversion for, what is true. In our head we would then have opinions that are wise and intelligent rather than foolish and dogmatic. And with our hands we would then act effectively and with freedom rather than in a self-defeating way.

This is why a common aim of psychotherapy is to facilitate the integration of our different fragmented selves into one self. Our previously separated feelings, thoughts, and actions can work together in one harmonious soul.

"Pythagoras said that ... if the healing art is most divine, it must occupy itself with the soul as well as with the body; for no creature can be sound so long as the higher part of it is sickly."
(Apollonius of Tyana – Greek philosopher)

Essentially a new and different harmony of heart, head and hands amounts to spiritual growth; a new will, new belief and new practice.

One example of this ideal integration is when we really care about someone then we really want to understand them and do things with them. The more clearly we understand them and the more we do together then the more deeply we care. Realising what their needs are, without doing anything to meet them due to lack of sympathy, reveals no linking of these three components.

This illustrates an important Swedenborgian principle - that influx adjusts itself according to efflux. In other words, what had been flowing out from us, as seen in our actions, will affect what feelings and thoughts flow into our hearts and heads. We can act on the good impulses and right ideas that come to us from the heavenly realm. As long as we are disposed to do what is good in the right way then this inflow can continue. However, if we do not act on these impulses we can only expect the inflow of good to hold itself back and eventually dry up altogether as we close the door to heaven within our soul.

A deeper way of speaking about this composition of the human being is to talk about spirit, mind and body. In other words, the three-sided idea addresses the spirituality of the divine spirit present within the individual's psychological and physical makeup.

As Krishna says:

"Strong are the senses; stronger than the senses is the mind; stronger than the mind is the understanding; but stronger than the understanding is the Spirit."
(*Bhagavad-Gita*, iii, 42 – Hindu tradition)

And Swedenborg:

"There is one single influx which is received by everyone according to his own disposition. This influx is an influx of affections from the Lord, from His mercy and life."
(Swedenborg. *Arcana Coelestia* Section 1285)

God

The notion we have of divine spirit is the deepest of all our ideas. Many think of God as divine spirit – the source of all selfless love and enlightenment. This divine spirit within our hearts and minds is what is humane in humanity - the spark of goodness inherent in many people who love their family and make personal sacrifices for the sake of those in need. We are also aware of its inner light guiding our useful individual response to the widely varied circumstances of life with which we have to deal.

The divine spirit also appears to link with forces and influences from outside of us e.g. inspiration for our creative thoughts, or uplift for our downcast mood. We also see the wonders of the material universe e.g. the laws of gravity that keep the planets predictably in their orbits and the incredible structure of the human body; an order within nature that many acknowledge could not have come about by mere chance, but rather through the activity of a higher creative power, independent of time and space.

There is thus a personal and a transcendent dimension to divine spirit. They are both necessary. We can be inwardly aware of the subjective dimension of God present within our private lives. At the same time, we have shared knowledge and understanding of the divine from an objective perspective that goes beyond what is private to the individual. This knowledge affects the meaning of individual experience. Because of these perceptions religious people believe in God. They worship him because they accept the need for divine inspiration and salvation.

God, like us, has heart, head and hands. This is not surprising as the Bible says we humans were created in his image. At heart, God is pure selfless love. In the head of God is the wisdom that knows and understands how to put that love into practice. In God's hands, there is power to act.

We can compare these three aspects of the divine spirit with the three aspects of every individual human being i.e. motivation, ideas and action. God's motivation has an end in view - the true happiness of all. His ideas are the wise principles revealed to us to bring about this end, and his action is the effect of these principles in the hearts and minds of people when they allow this.

We can only have an obscure idea of God but we have a better understanding by relating to God's human side; for we can see divine love, wisdom and action in the life of Jesus. We can learn about and relate, person to person, to divine humanity.

> *"God the Father...is invisible, and therefore unapproachable and incapable of being linked to man. That is why He came into the world, and made Himself visible, approachable and capable of being linked. ....For unless in approaching God we think about Him as a man, all ideas about God are vain; they collapse like the power of sight directed towards the universe, that is, into empty space."*
> (Swedenborg. *True Christian Religion* Section 538)

This is the God with whom we can get on a personal footing whilst realising we can never be divine of ourselves. Nevertheless, as we do so, we can also feel the divine spirit actively present within our souls inspiring and guiding our lives.

Spiritual World

- The spiritual world inspires our creative ideas and negative moods and also tempts us to wrong-doing.

- It is the realm of which we become clearly conscious after bodily death, when we will no longer be distracted by sensations from the world. It is as real and tangible as the physical universe, if not more so. Whatever is seen is a projection of the inner states of thought and feeling of its inhabitants. Those who are mainly good at heart, having the true light of heavenly wisdom, will see beautiful representations of their inner states of mind. However, those who are mainly bad at heart, having only the misleading light of self-intelligence will usually see illusory representations of their thoughts and wishes; images that disguise the ugliness of their hellish state of mind. The reason for this is things appear, not due to physical laws, but rather due to what corresponds to the human mind.

- The spiritual world is thus the world where spirits live. These are either lovely or horrible people who once lived on earth. During our altered states of consciousness we have an extra-sensory perception of their presence and activity. We may see their appearance, hear their voices or be aware of imagery representing their condition. Many, including Swedenborg, have witnessed this with varying degrees of clarity.

- The spiritual world is also our own unconscious mind at work where all our feelings and thoughts originate. It is responsible for all our many thoughts, impulses, and sentiments that are on the edge of consciousness. Unknown to them and us, we attract higher and lower spirits according to what we desire and then we experience their life within our own hearts and minds.

Spiritual Growth

How can we each develop as people so that we overcome our frailties, imperfections and problems? What is the process by which change takes place?

In different chapters, I have tried to write about various aspects of this process. However, the following is my attempt at summarising this psycho-spiritual material in what I believe to be an answer to this question.

There is no straight line of development but rather countless cycles, each one dealing with a different facet of our lives. In order for spiritual growth to become possible there needs to be a change of heart and mind – a turning around. This might seem like our sacrificing the current way of life with its pleasures and relationships. However, a useful idea of sacrifice is a making whole. The spiritually immature attitude to sacrifice is giving something away in order to get something we want. A different attitude is letting go of one's sense of separateness from others, one's concern for self, one's preoccupation with time and material matters. To transcend from a lower level to a higher level, one has to stop identifying oneself with the lower level. For example, the individual who collects facts about the world can let go of this obsession and instead reflect rationally on what is interesting. If we were really to grow spiritually, it would be through refraining from doing what is less useful and becoming more engaged in a fulfilling social role.

Each cycle appears to have several steps.

Knowledge

Our senses mislead us into assuming that only the natural and social world around us exists. Through them we look at the outer and do not notice the inner. Trying to meet our own bodily and social needs in terms of the external things around us, we have yet to find any deeper meaning to our lives. Yet, the divine spirit can help us notice a glimmer of a difference between the outward and inward things of life. In other words to find meaning one needs first to have a knowledge about oneself and life. Required is an interest in coming to know something deeper about oneself and things about life that might involve discomfort in their discovery. The psycho-spiritual approach to self-knowledge is partly to do with learning about how one can recognise personal problems. We can contrast an attitude of seeking to know about oneself with a lack of interest in self-knowing or only a superficial and egotistic curiosity about oneself.

Understanding

Understanding goes further than knowledge. It is appreciating what causes what in one's life and how things are connected together. The understanding gained about human functioning and relationships can come via many sources e.g. one's parents, friends, counsellor, and from spiritual books. Merely knowing about these ideas is a matter of the gathering of information, whereas developing a clear grasp involves exercising one's intuitive and rational mind. We start to think of ourselves in terms of this new insight, seeing some of what is lower and higher within our own thoughts. We also begin to appreciate some value in the latter.

Acknowledgement

It is not enough to understand why we have the problems we have, e.g. how our fears result in the trouble we get into. The individual needs also to admit where he or she is going wrong and to acknowledge the need for personal change and the responsibility for making this change. Those higher values we have recognised challenge our egocentric ways. We acknowledge to ourselves our mistakes and errors and draw on what we have learned to develop our own ideas of what are better ways.

Acceptance

Knowledge, understanding and acknowledgment are of the head. However the heart is important too.

"He who wants to obtain true faith must know, because faith grows out of spiritual knowledge. The faith that comes from that knowledge is rooted in the heart."
(Paracelsus. *De Fundamento Sapientae* – Swiss occultist)

Unless there is a change of heart, we can retract something that we had only acknowledged in the mind the previous day. We may have recognised where we are going wrong, but what is crucially important is an emotional acceptance of a way forward. Religion and psychotherapy are about personal change if they are about anything.

Psychotherapists talk about resistance by the patient to making personal change because of self-insights that remain only on an intellectual level. Emotional acceptance of what change is needed is more of a wrench than mere acknowledgment because it means real acceptance of the consequences of giving up old ways, old pleasures and old attitudes. Fully to accept an uncomfortable point about oneself requires courage. Any about-turn involves a heartfelt conversion. It means accepting in our hearts that any good we can do is inspired from God and any right thinking we have results from him illuminating our minds.

Resolve and Effort

Despite accepting the need for change, we may yet still be tardy in going about change. This is due to a lack of resolve. It is one thing to face in a new direction but another to set off with a will. We try to follow our conscience but find that life tests us by real choices and our motives for change are less than pure. We experience some resistance. We may do what is good and useful because it is the right thing to do, rather than because this is what we really want to do. The way forward does not seem as clear now we have mixed motives. However, when the light that had come from a strong desire to change fades, there is still some dim light in our understanding that we call upon. Without a firm intention on the part of the individual, no personal transformation can take place. When one finds oneself in a tempting situation, then one's degree of determination is really tested. Unless there is an inner fight and struggle to follow the new pattern, the person can easily backslide. This means fighting against what is undesirable within us.

Surrender

In the end we realise we cannot win the battle unaided. The alcoholic surrenders to the higher power to beat the demon drink because he or she accepts that the battle cannot be won through one's own efforts alone. Likewise, when the going gets really tough and we realise we are just not strong enough for the fight, we all need humbly to ask for help. We may trust that God can help us because he is the source of all that is good and true. There is a paradox here of needing to be both active and passive at the same time; active in seeking help and following divine leadership and passive in surrendering the outcome to the power of divine spirit. In turning to the higher values we have come to believe in – rather than our old self-oriented desires – we find our heart strengthened as a new love is now active in what we do.

Rest

We no longer have to struggle to overcome this aspect of our own love of self or love of worldly pleasure. We understand what is right because we perceive what is good. What is true joins with what is good in us. For a while, we may feel satisfied, anxiety-free and in a state of inner happiness.

Summary

In Swedenborg's terminology, these steps involve repentance, reformation and regeneration. Repentance is to do with wanting to change from ways of living that are recognised as unsatisfactory and self-defeating. Reformation is focusing the mind on new ways of thinking about better ways of living. Regeneration is following the new ideas e.g. having a heart-felt concern to lead a useful life rather than one dominated by self-interest so that the right ways of behaving become second nature; a new character from God in each of us, replacing our old desires with a new set.

One cycle involving these elements is not enough to transform our character which has many sides to it. We need to travel through the cycle repeatedly, each time in relation to a different aspect of ourselves. Gradually, as we do so, we ascend the spiritual ladder. Our whole being can be transformed from one who falls for the illusions of a self-oriented way of life to one who is associated with a heavenly sense of peace, contentment and joy.

What is good in the heart and true in the head are then in harmony. The result is a heavenly state within the person; the heavenly marriage of goodness and truth with its offspring the life of doing what is good and useful on a daily basis.

"Purification from evils and falsities consists in refraining from them, steering clear of them, and loathing them; the implantation of goodness and truth consists in thinking and willing what is good and what is true, and in speaking and doing them; and the joining together of the two consists in leading a life composed of them. For when the good and truth residing with a person have been joined together his will is new and his understanding is new, consequently his life is new. When this is how a person is, divine worship is present in every deed he performs; for at every point the person now has what is divine in view, respects and loves it, and in so doing worships it."

(Swedenborg. *Arcana Coelestia* Section 10143[3])

Worship is present in every deed.

163

Chapter Notes

1. Introduction

1 For a brief summary regarding Emanuel Swedenborg's life, see:

- Swedenborg Explores the Spiritual Dimension. Kingslake, Brian. pages 17-26 Seminar Books 1981
- Emanuel Swedenborg: Essential Readings. Stanley, Michael. North Atlantic Books 1988 pages 15-25.

For biographies:

- Swedenborg's Secret: a biography. Bergquist, Lars. The Swedenborg Society 2005
- Emanuel Swedenborg: Visionary Savant in the Age of Reason. Benz, Ernst. (translated by N Goodridge-Clarke) Swedenborg Foundation 2002
- Swedenborg Epic: The life and works of Emanuel Swedenborg. Sigstedt, Cyriel Odhner. Bookman Associates: 1952

2 For further information on Swedenborg's writings concerning correspondences, see The Language of Parable. Worcester, William L. Swedenborg Press New York 1976

3 Regarding double-aspect terms see The Psychology of Religious Knowing. by Watts, F & Williams, M. Cambridge University Press 1988 page 8

2. Looking for Answers

1 See L Tolstoy, My Confession, My Religion, The Gospel in Brief 1929 New York: Charles Scribner, Pages 12-14.

2 For further information on Swedenborg's teaching regarding the love of truth, the divine within and enlightenment see:

- Emanuel Swedenborg: Essential Readings. Stanley, Michael. North Atlantic Books 1988 Chapter 4 on the divine in Man and Chapter 7 on Rebirth
- Returning to the Source Van Dusen, Wilson. Real People Press 1996
- Uses: A Way of Personal and Spiritual Growth. Van Dusen, Wilson. Swedenborg Foundation 1981

3. Taking the Initiative

1 For further information on Swedenborg's teaching regarding freedom, proprium and regeneration see:

- The Joy of Spiritual Growth: Real Encounters. Rose, Frank & Maginel, Bob. Swedenborg Foundation 1999
- Eve the Bone of Contention. Stanley, Michael. Seminar Books 1992
- The Doctrine of the Proprium. De Charms, George. General Church Book Center Bryn Athyn Pennsylvania 1987
- True Christian Religion. Swedenborg, Emanuel. Swedenborg Society translated 1988 Chapter 6 on faith and chapter 9 on repentance

2 See Reality Therapy by William Glasser, Harper Collins 1989

3 This case description is provided by William James in The Varieties of Religious Experience. 1902 Centenary Edition Routledge, in the chapter on conversion.

4. Valuing Sex

1 For further information on Swedenborg's writings concerning chaste sexuality and conjugial love see:

- Emanuel Swedenborg: Essential Readings. Stanley, Michael. North Atlantic Books 1988 Chapter 10 Sexuality and the Conjugial Relationship
- Conjugial Love. Swedenborg, Emanuel. Translated by John Chadwick. The Swedenborg Society 1996 Chapter 7 Chastity and Unchastity

- Emanuel Swedenborg: Visionary Savant in the Age of Reason. Benz, Ernst. Translated by N Goodridge-Clarke. Swedenborg Foundation 2002 pages 406-424
- Rise Above It: Spiritual Development through the Ten Commandments. Silverman, Ray and Silverman, Star. Touchstone Seminars 2000

5. Working on Love

1 For further information on Swedenborg's writings concerning coldness in marriage and conjugial love see:

- Emanuel Swedenborg: Essential Readings. Stanley, Michael. North Atlantic Books 1988 Chapter 10 Sexuality and the Conjugial Relationship
- Conjugial Love. Swedenborg, Emanuel. Translated by John Chadwick. The Swedenborg Society 1996 Chapter 11 The Reasons for Coldness, Separation and Divorce in Marriage
- Emanuel Swedenborg: Visionary Savant in the Age of Reason. Benz, Ernst. Swedenborg Foundation 2002 Pages 406-424

2 For example see The Good Marriage: How and Why Love Lasts by Wallerstein, J. S. & Blakeslee, S. 1995 Boston: Houghton Mifflin

6. Being Acceptable

1 For example see the opening chapter in Existential Psychology Edited by Rollo May 2nd Edition 1969 Random House

2 For an introduction to Jung's idea of the collective unconscious and its archetypes see A Critical Dictionary of Jungian Analysis by Andrew Samuels, Bani Shorter & Fred Plaut 1986 Routledge

3 For an introduction to Swedenborg's teaching on the spiritual world see Emanuel Swedenborg: Essential Readings. Michael Stanley. North Atlantic Books 1988 Chapter 9 deals with Swedenborg's concept of the spiritual world.

4 For further information on Swedenborg's teaching regarding the divine human within see:

- Swedenborg Explores the Spiritual Dimension. Kingslake, Brian. Seminar Books 1981 Chapter 13 on the Divine Human
- True Christian Religion. Swedenborg, Emanuel. Swedenborg Society translated 1988 Chapters 2 and 3

7. Gaining Self-Control

1 For further information on Swedenborg's teaching regarding faith and natural and spiritual temptations see:

- Psychology as Servant of Religion. Grange, Alan. Seminar Books 1970 Section 4 on spiritual conflict
- The New Jerusalem and its Heavenly Doctrine. Swedenborg, Emanuel. Swedenborg Society Section 187-195 on temptation

8. Finding Forgiveness

1 Much has been written concerning psychoanalysis. I have found an excellent introduction to be Freud and the Post-Freudians. J A C Brown Penguin 1964 edition

2 This is the inspiring and profoundly moving story of Ken and Treya Wilber told in the book Grace and Grit by Ken Wilber Gateway 2nd Edition 2001.

3 For further information on Swedenborg's teaching regarding conscience, repentance and faith see:

- Emanuel Swedenborg: Essential Readings. Stanley, Michael. North Atlantic Books 1988 Chapter 3 on Man's Nature
- Psychology as Servant of Religion. Grange, Alan. Seminar Books 1970 Section 12 on Guidance
- The New Jerusalem and its Heavenly Doctrine Swedenborg, Emanuel. Swedenborg Society Section 9 on Conscience, Section 11 on Merit and Section 12 on Repentance and the Forgiveness of Sins

9. Calming Anger

1 For a Western view and description of Eastern world religion I have found the following book to be clear and illuminating The Religious Experience of Mankind. Ninian Smart. Fontana 1969

2 The Rainbow People of God: by Archbishop Desmond Tutu edited by John Allen. Doubleday 1994

3 For further information on Swedenborg's teaching regarding a charitable heart and the proprium see:

- Returning to the Source. Van Dusen, Wilson. Real People Press 1996
- The New Jerusalem and its Heavenly Doctrine. Swedenborg, Emanuel. Swedenborg Society Chapter 6 on love towards the neighbour.
- Eve the Bone of Contention. Stanley, Michael. Seminar Books 1992 Pages 17-18 and 59-68 on psyche and ego,
- Emanuel Swedenborg: Essential Readings. Stanley, Michael. North Atlantic Books 1988 Chapter 3 on man's nature and chapter 8 on angelic nature

10. Valuing What we Do

1 For information on Abraham Maslow's theory of deficiency and growth motives see any good Psychology Textbook such as Psychology for A2 level by Mike Cardwell, Liz Clark and Claire Meldrum 2004 Harper-Collins

2 For further information on Swedenborg's teaching regarding usefulness and mutual love see:

- Uses: A Way of Personal and Spiritual Growth. Van Dusen, Wilson. Swedenborg Foundation 1981
- Charity: The Practice of Neighborliness. Swedenborg, Emanuel. Translated by W. Wunsch. Swedenborg Foundation

11. Facing our Flaws

1 Psychotherapist Eric Berne (Games People Play: The Psychology of Human Relationships, Berne, E. 1964, Penguin Books) contends that three undesirable (and unconscious) needs motivate 'games' between people which actually interfere with finding friendships, love, and closeness.

2 Carl Jung wrote about our 'shadow' defined as the repressed characteristics of the ego. see A Critical Dictionary of Jungian Analysis by Andrew Samuels, Bani Shorter & Fred Plaut 1986 Routledge

3 See The Islamist by Ed Husain Penguin 2007

4 For Swedenborg's teaching regarding conscience see: Essential Swedenborg Section 132 on conscience

5 For Swedenborg's teaching on self-judgment, regeneration and repentance see:

- Swedenborg Explores the Spiritual Dimension. Kingslake, Brian. Seminar Books 1981 Chapter 8 on self-judgment
- Emanuel Swedenborg: Essential Readings. Stanley, Michael. North Atlantic Books 1988 Chapter 7 on regeneration

12. Feeling Good about Oneself

1 For further information on Swedenborg's teaching regarding human fallen nature see:

- Emanuel Swedenborg: Essential Readings. Stanley, Michael. North Atlantic Books 1988 Chapter 3 on man's nature.
- Swedenborg: Buddha of the North Suzuki, D T. Swedenborg Foundation 1996 Pages 92-101 The concept of the self and the love of self

2 Swedenborg writing about the spirit and merit of God can be seen in The New Jerusalem and its Heavenly Doctrine Swedenborg, Emanuel. Swedenborg Society Sections 150-157

3 The psychoanalyst Erich Fromm points out that the idea that Freud is against religion is misleading unless we define sharply what religion or what aspects of religion he is critical of and

what aspects of religion he speaks for. See Psychoanalysis and Religion. Erich Fromm 1950 Yale University Press New Haven & London

13. Asking for Help
1 Psychologist Gordon W. Allport described both the extrinsic and intrinsic orientations Personality and Social Encounter: Selected Essays. Boston: Beacon Press, 1960 pp 257-267
2 This case description of David is provided by William James in The Varieties of Religious Experience 1902 Centenary Edition Routledge, in the chapter on conversion.
3 For further information on Swedenborg's teaching regarding the nature of God and prayer see Swedenborg Explores the Spiritual Dimension. Kingslake, Brian. Seminar Books 1981 Chapter 17 on prayer

14. Learning to Trust
1 For a practical application of Swedenborg's teaching regarding charity see The Joy of Spiritual Growth: Real Encounters. Rose, Frank & Maginel, Bob. Swedenborg Foundation 1999
2 The Act of Will: Self-Actualisation through Psychosynthesis. by Roberto Assagioli 1973 Aquarian/Thorsons HarperCollins

15. Attaining Peace of Mind
1 See Synchronicity: An Acausal Connecting Principle by C G Jung translated by R F C Hull Princeton/Bollingen Edition 1973 Extracted from the Structure and Dynamics of the Psyche, Vol 8 of the collected works.
2 For further information on Swedenborg's doctrine of divine providence see Emanuel Swedenborg: Essential Readings. Stanley, Michael. North Atlantic Books 1988   Chapter 6 on divine providence
3 Quoted in The Confidence Plan by Sarah Litvinoff BBC Active 2004

16. Dealing with Death
1 See Life After Life by Moody, Raymond Jr. Atlanta: Mockingbird Books, 1975
2 For further information on Swedenborg's teaching regarding judgement and the spiritual world see:
   * Tunnel to Eternity: Beyond near-death. Rhodes, Leon. Chrysalis Books 1997
   * Window to Eternity. Henderson, Bruce. Swedenborg Foundation 1987
   * The Shorter Heaven and Hell. Emanuel Swedenborg. Abridged by Moffat, T and Duckworth, J. Seminar Books 1994
3 See Is there an Afterlife? by David Fontana 2006 O Books

17. Surviving a Catastrophe
1 See Man's Search for meaning: An Introduction to Logotherapy by Frankl, Viktor Translated by I Lasch Beacon Press 1962
2 Psychosynthesis : A Manual of Principles and Techniques 1965 by Assagioli, R., Aquarian/ Thorsons HarperCollins
3 For further information on Swedenborg's teaching regarding God's permission of disorder, natural and spiritual temptation, proprium and regeneration see:
   * Emanuel Swedenborg: Essential Readings. Stanley, Michael. North Atlantic Books 1988 On temptation combat in chapter 7 and in chapter 6 on divine providence.
   * Divine Providence. Swedenborg, Emanuel. Swedenborg Society Sections 275-284 on permission of evil
   * Personal Revelation. Stanley, Michael. The Swedenborg Open Learning Centre 2006 Pages 41-72 on causes of spiritual decline, and revelation of ego destructiveness
   * Eve the Bone of Contention. Stanley, Michael. Seminar Books 1992

- The Doctrine of the Proprium. De Charms, George. General Church Book Center Bryn Athyn Pennsylvania 1987

4 Vera Von der Heydt gives expression to the Jungian view of a dark side to the God-image in Prospects for the Soul: Soundings in Jungian Psychology and Religion by Von der Heydt, V. 1976 Darton, Longman & Todd page53

18. Coming to Terms with Voices

1 This experience is described by William James in The Varieties of Religious Experience. 1902 Centenary Edition Routledge, in the chapter on the reality of the unseen.

2 Touching the Void by J. Simpson 1988 Pan Books

3 See:
- The Natural Depth in Man. Van Dusen, Wilson. Swedenborg Foundation 1972
- The Presence of Other Worlds. Van Dusen, Wilson. Swedenborg Foundation 1974

4 For further information on Swedenborg's teaching regarding the presence of spirits from the spiritual world see Heaven and Hell Swedenborg, Emanuel. Swedenborg Society Section 291 – 302

19. Shaking off Unhappy Moods

1 The Psychology of Religious Belief by Pratt J B, 1907 Macmillan; New York

2 See Van Dusen's books:
- The Natural Depth in Man. Van Dusen, Wilson. Swedenborg Foundation 1972
- The Presence of Other Worlds. Van Dusen, Wilson. Swedenborg Foundation 1974

20. Reacting to Wrongdoers

1 For further information on Swedenborg's teaching regarding punishment and self-judgment see:
- Essential Swedenborg. Synnesvedt, Sig. Swedenborg Foundation 1977 Part 1
- True Christian Religion. Swedenborg, Emanuel. Swedenborg Society translated 1988 Section 498 on free-will.

21. Overcoming Obsessions

1 An Angel at my Shoulder: True stories of angelic experiences. Eckersley, Glennyce. Rider Books 1996

22. Discovering Confidence

1 See Toward a Psychology of Being by A.H. Maslow 2nd Edition 1968 Van Nostrand Reinhold Company

2 For further information on Swedenborg's teaching regarding the Universal Human (often translated as the Grand Man) and the Good of Usefulness see:
- Emanuel Swedenborg: Essential Readings. Stanley, Michael. North Atlantic Books 1988 Chapter 9 on the Spiritual World.
- Uses: A Way of Personal and Spiritual Growth. Van Dusen, Wilson. Swedenborg Foundation 1981
- The Joy of Spiritual Growth: Real Encounters. Rose, Frank & Maginel, Bob. Swedenborg Foundation 1999

23. Living through Crisis

1 For further information on Swedenborg's teaching regarding deeper psycho-spiritual changes associated with personal growth see Personal Revelation. Stanley, Michael. The Swedenborg Open Learning Centre 2006

2 Psychosynthesis : A Manual of Principles and Techniques 1965 by Assagioli, R., Aquarian/ Thorsons HarperCollins

24. Receiving Hope through Despair

1 Arcana Coelestia. Emanuel Swedenborg Translated by John Elliot Swedenborg Society section 2694

2 For further information on Swedenborg's teaching regarding spiritual influx and temptation combat see:

- Emanuel Swedenborg: Essential Readings. Stanley, Michael. North Atlantic Books 1988 Chapter 7 on regeneration
- Existentialism and the New Christianity. Barnitz, Harry. Philosophical Library Inc. 1969 Chapter 5 on angst
- The New Jerusalem and its Heavenly Doctrine. Swedenborg, Emanuel. Swedenborg Society Sections 187 – 195 on temptation.

25. Drawing Ideas Together

1 For further information on Swedenborg's holistic approach to psychology, philosophy and theology see:

- Swedenborg's Religious Psychology. James, Leon in Studia Swedenborgiana, Vol. 8, Dec. 1993, Number 3, pages 13-42.
- The Golden Thread: Spiritual and Mental Health. Childs, Geoffrey S. General Church Publication Committee Bryn Athyn, Pennsylvania
- Psychology as Servant of Religion. Grange, Alan. Seminar Books 1970

Selected Reading

A Book about Dying Gives a Swedenborgian view of the afterlife from the author's perspective of the day to day realities of caring for a terminally ill wife. Presents the spiritual experiences of the dying and of the survivors, showing that for patient and survivor alike, living really does continue after dying.
Kirven, Robert. Swedenborg Foundation 1997 ISBN 0-87785-175-1

A Psychology of Spiritual Healing The principles described are revealed in a range of interests that will have an impact on the psychology of health and consciousness.
Taylor, Eugine. Chrysalis books 1997 ISBN 0-87785-375-4

An Angel at my Shoulder True stories of angelic experiences.
Eckersley, Glennyce. Rider Books 1996 ISBN 0-7126-7208-7

Angels in Action: What Swedenborg Saw and Heard Swedenborg's visions and the meaning they can have in our lives are explained. Also shown is how angels work for us from birth through death and how we can be angels on earth.
Kirven, Robert H. Chrysalis Books 1994 ISBN 0-87785-147-6

Arcana Coelestia This is Swedenborg's largest work. It is a profound psycho-spiritual interpretation of the first two books of the Bible. It also contains description and discussion of various matters that religiously-minded people may wish to know.
Swedenborg, Emanuel. Translated by John Elliott in 12 volumes. The Swedenborg Society 1983-1999 ISBN 0-85448-089-7 etc.
Available on-line at http://www.theheavenlydoctrines.org/static/d8086/1.htm

Charity: The Practice of Neighborliness Practical book for compassionate living providing the tools of responsible service.
Swedenborg, Emanuel. 1766 Translated by W. Wunsch. Swedenborg Foundation
ISBN 0-87785-145-X

Conjugial Love Few books have been written that could claim to cover comprehensively the relationship between the sexes. This is such a book.
Swedenborg, Emanuel. Translated by John Chadwick. The Swedenborg Society 1996
ISBN 0-85448-122-2

Divine Love and Wisdom Shows how God's love, wisdom and humanity are reflected in creation and in ourselves and suggests that the act of Creation is not a mystery of the past, but a miracle ongoing in every instant of the present.
Swedenborg, Emanuel. Swedenborg Foundation Translated by George F. Dole 2003 ISBN 0987785-481-5

Divine Providence God governs his creation through divine providence. To be in full harmony with divine providence, the human will and the human understanding must be in accord with the order of creation. Providence looks to the preservation of this order although human free-will may violate it.
Swedenborg, Emanuel. Swedenborg Society 1764 ISBN 978-0-85448-036-4
Available on-line at http://www.theheavenlydoctrines.org/static/d15083/1.htm

Emanuel Swedenborg: Essential Readings. Arranged by subject and carefully explained, this excellent book makes the range and depth of Swedenborg's ideas accessible to the modern reader seeking to grasp holistically the physical and spiritual dimensions of life.
Stanley, Michael. North Atlantic Books 1988 ISBN 1-55643-467-7

Emanuel Swedenborg: Visionary Savant in the Age of Reason (translated by N Goodridge-Clarke) Offers what has been said to be the best access to Swedenborg's thought. Provides biographical material and covers some of the main teachings in the context of philosophical and esoteric ideas.
Benz, Ernst. Swedenborg Foundation 2002 ISBN 0-87785-195-6

Essential Swedenborg Summarises in modern terms the basic features of the theology.
Synnesvedt, Sig. Swedenborg Foundation 1977 ISBN 0-87785-152-2

Eve the Bone of Contention A psychospiritual understanding of the story of Creation and the Garden of Eden.
Stanley, Michael. Seminar Books 1992 ISBN 0-907295-19-3

Existentialism and the New Christianity Deals with Swedenborg's teachings in relation to such topics as essence and existence, freedom, the self, angst, suffering etc.
Barnitz, Harry. Philosophical Library Inc. 1969
Library of Congress Catalog Card Number 69-14353

Heaven and Hell (The full version) A description based on things heard and seen; we are shown how we enter the next world; the spiritual character of our surroundings there; where and how judgment is effected; the life of heaven; the training of children; marriage; etc. these and many other matters are described in great detail.
Swedenborg, Emanuel. Swedenborg Society 1758 ISBN 0 85448 051
Available free on-line at http://swedenborg.newearth.org/hh/hh00toc.html

Into the Interior: Discovering Swedenborg. The author presents a stimulating and at times provocative insight into Swedenborg's ideas of mysticism, sexuality, radicalism and their relevance to contemporary thought.
Lachman, Gary. The Swedenborg Society 2006 ISBN 0-85448-149-4

Personal Revelation: A guide to a personal interpretation of the book of Revelation Those who have known what St John of the Cross termed 'the dark night of the soul' could well find a helpful and comforting light of understanding drawn from Swedenborg's insights.
Stanley, Michael. The Swedenborg Open Learning Centre 2006

Psychology as Servant of Religion Provides a short introduction to the psychology of Swedenborg. Grange, Alan. Seminar Books 1970

Returning to the Source Discusses shifts in outlook and understanding in terms of mystery and awe, the nature of the spiritual, and personal relationship to the divine.
Van Dusen, Wilson. Real People Press 1996 ISBN 0-911226-37-0

Rise Above It: Spiritual Development through the Ten Commandments Filled with candour and inspiring journal entries from seminar participants, this book invites us to enter into a life of increasing love, wisdom and service.
Silverman, Ray and Silverman, Star. Touchstone Seminars 2000 ISBN 0-9670768-0-3

Swedenborg: Buddha of the North This book provides an accessible overview and introduction to Emanual Swedenborg. It provides the author's perceptive comparisons between Buddhism and Swedenborg's views.
Suzuki, D T. Swedenborg Foundation 1996 ISBN 0-87785-184-0

Swedenborg Explores the Spiritual Dimension A personal and succinct summary of what the author describes as a 'pre-digested version' of Swedenborg's main teachings.
Kingslake, Brian. Seminar Books 1981 ISBN 0-949463-04-3

Swedenborg's Religious Psychology: The Marriage of Good and Truth as Mental Health Leon James, psychologist, discusses the three-fold terminology used in Swedenborg's theology, philosophy and psychology.
James, Leon in Studia Swedenborgiana, Vol. 8, Dec. 1993, Number 3, Pages 13-42

Swedenborg's Secret: a Biography Connects Swedenborg's many ideas with the different paths and events of his private and public life. Likely to be the standard biography for the foreseeable future.
Bergquist, Lars. The Swedenborg Society 2005 ISBN 0-85448-143-5

The Doctrine of the Proprium Describes how the selfhood of the individual develops from childhood to old age and how the spiritual mind develops.
De Charms, George. General Church Book Center Bryn Athyn Pennsylvania 1987

The Golden Thread: Spiritual and Mental Health Addresses key personal questions to do with individual identity, origin of feelings and thoughts and the purpose of life by clarifying philosophical concepts in lay language and drawing together psychological discoveries and teachings from Swedenborg's writings that make sense to the rational mind.
Childs, Geoffrey S. General Church Publication Committee Bryn Athyn, Pennsylvania ISBN 0-910557-15-2

The Joy of Spiritual Growth: Real Encounters An account of a spiritual growth group programme applying the principles of Emanuel Swedenborg's theology and a twelve-step approach. Participants share their struggles in their own words as they work towards more meaningful relationships with God, self and others, as they learn how to forgive, to release false cause and to live in the present.
Rose, Frank & Maginel, Bob. Swedenborg Foundation 1999 ISBN 0-87785-384-3

The Language of Parable The book shows Swedenborg's description of how earthly terms used in our speech and in nature correspond to inner human qualities. This appreciation of the way the natural echoes the spiritual, throws new light on the deeper significance of the Bible.
Worcester, William L. Swedenborg Press New York 1976 ISBN 0-87785-155-7

The Natural Depth in Man A clinical psychologist pieces together clues drawn from his own personal experience, his work with emotionally disturbed people, and his study of philosophy to guide us through the secret spaces of the inner world.
Van Dusen, Wilson. Swedenborg Foundation 1972 ISBN 0-87785-165-4

The New Jerusalem and its Heavenly Doctrine Swedenborg presents summaries of a number of doctrines developed in greater length in other theological writings.
Swedenborg, Emanuel. Swedenborg Society 1757-1758. ISBN 0-85448-112-5
Available on-line as The Heavenly City: A Spiritual Guidebook at
http://swedenborg.newearth.org/hcsg/

The Presence of Other Worlds This volume is the account of the frightening journey of Swedenborg through the depth of his own mind to the spirit world beyond and back again. The author, a clinical psychologist, presents Swedenborg's dreams and visions to show how personal inner spiritual exploration, psychic experience and the spirit realm are connected together.
Van Dusen, Wilson. Swedenborg Foundation 1974 ISBN 0-87785-166-2

The Shorter Heaven and Hell A sixth of the length of the original, this abridged version still retains the essential ideas of the longer work covering Swedenborg's insightful and thorough analysis of his own extraordinary experiences in the spirit world.
Abridged by Moffat, T and Duckworth, J. Seminar Books 1994 ISBN 0-907295-20-7

The Swedenborg Epic: The Life and Works of Emanuel Swedenborg Tells in chronological order the story of Swedenborg's life as it unfolds and as it appeared to his contemporaries.
Sigstedt, Cyriel Odhner. Bookman Associates: 1952

True Christian Religion Gives a complete and connected exposition of the Doctrine of the New Church, Swedenborg, Emanuel. Swedenborg Society translated 1988 ISBN 1-85448-105-2

Tunnel to Eternity: Beyond Near-Death This book provides an illuminating Swedenborgian perspective on the NDE and the entire afterlife journey that it promises. It shows the spiritual world into which the NDE itself is just the briefest glimpse.
Rhodes, Leon. Chrysalis Books 1997 ISBN 0-87785-378-9

Uses: A Way of Personal and Spiritual Growth.
Van Dusen, Wilson. Swedenborg Foundation 1981

Window to Eternity One of the best works to explain Swedenborg's conception of the afterlife.
Henderson, Bruce. Swedenborg Foundation ISBN 0-87785-132-8

More Swedenborgian Sources

Free On-line Materials
- The Spiritual Wisdom Web Site provides various free introductory articles on-line to help explain the meaning of our lives using Swedenborg's insights.
  http://www.spiritualwisdom.org.uk/
- The Swedenborg Channel has free short videos about Swedenborg, his ideas, heaven, science illuminating the world of spirit.
  http://www.newcenturytv.com/swedenborg/
- Swedenborg's original books in English translation are freely available on the internet at:
  - Swedenborg Digital Library http://www.swedenborgproject.org/
  - The Heavenly Doctrines http://www.theheavenlydoctrines.org/.
  - Small Canon Search http://smallcanonsearch.com/
  - New Earth http://swedenborg.newearth.org/

Leaflets and Magazines
The Swedenborg Movement publishes leaflets and a magazine Outlook available free of charge, 20-21 Bloomsbury Way London WC1A 2TH. Articles are available on-line at
http://www.swedenborgmovement.org/

Courses
Purley Chase is a residential centre in the English Midlands providing spiritual retreat and conference facilities for reflection and learning in relation to Swedenborgian ideas.
http://www.purleychasecentre.org.uk/
The Swedenborg Open Learning Centre (SOLCe) is based in England and provides distance learning courses including group tutorials for study of Swedenborg's psycho-spiritual principles and their personal and pastoral application. http://www.swedenborg-openlearning.org.uk/

Bookstores
The original writings of Swedenborg in translation and other books containing his ideas are available through the following booksellers
The Swedenborg Society 20-21 Bloomsbury Way London WC1A 2TH United Kingdom
http://www.swedenborg.org.uk/
North of England New Church House 34 John Dalton Street Manchester M2 6LE
The Swedenborg Foundation Chrysalis Books 320 North Church Street West Chester PA 19380
U.S.A. http://www.swedenborg.com
Information Swedenborg Inc 279 Burnamthorpe Road Toronto Ontario Canada M9B 1Z6
http://www.swedenborg.ca
Second hand copies can often be obtained through non-specialist online book stores such as
http://www.amazon.co.uk

Religious Groups using Swedenborgian Ideas
The General Conference of the New Church is a British organisation of religious church groups who consider Swedenborg's writings to be divinely inspired, enabling a modern understanding of the Bible. http://www.generalconference.org.uk/
Swedenborgian Church of North America This organisation of church groups says it is an open-minded, forward looking Christian church drawing its faith from the Bible as illuminated by the teachings of Emanuel Swedenborg http://www.swedenborg.org/
General Church of the New Jerusalem a USA-based organisation of church groups that also provides free on-line audio and text material based on Swedenborg's teachings.
http://www.newchurch.org/sermons

Index

addiction, 29, 40, 79, 111, 151
adultery, 33, 62, 129, 131
adulthood, 56, 82, 134, 141
affection, 34, 37, 38, 41, 47, 71, 81, 106, 126
afterlife, 101, 102, 104, 167, 170, 173
aimlessness, 140
alienation, 151
Allport, Gordon W, 167
anger, 7, 8, 9, 41, 64, 65, 66, 67, 68, 69, 71, 74, 77, 93, 108, 113
anxiety, 7, 8, 74, 95, 96, 97, 112, 133, 135, 140, 145, 149, 162
apartheid, 65
apparitions, 119, 121
archetypal images, 45, 113
Assagioli, Roberto, 93, 112, 146, 167, 168
association of ideas, 118
attributions, 61, 82, 100, 136
Barnitz, Harry, 169, 171
beliefs, 8, 10, 15, 18, 20, 21, 22, 24, 25, 27, 34, 35, 41, 46, 47, 48, 49, 52, 53, 54, 60, 61, 65, 67, 69, 73, 75, 76, 78, 79, 82, 83, 85, 86, 87, 90, 91, 97, 99, 100, 101, 104, 106, 107, 111, 112, 113, 114, 117, 120, 121, 126, 130, 132, 134, 135, 139, 147, 150, 151, 152, 153, 156, 158, 159, 162, 168
disbelief, 108
Benz, Ernst, 164, 165, 171
bereavement, 108, 122
Bergquist, Lars, 164, 172
Berne, Eric, 74, 75, 166
Bible, 48, 51, 75, 85, 113, 114, 158, 170, 172, 174
Blakeslee, S, 165
blame, 22, 60, 65, 82, 83, 93, 145
boredom, 70
Bowlby, J., 47
brainstorming, 13
breathing, 15, 19
Brown, J A C, 165
Buddhism, 25, 54, 57, 67, 94, 109
Cardwell, Mike, 166
catastrophe, 109, 110, 111, 112, 139
Chadwick, John, 164, 165, 170
character, 10, 28, 44, 49, 53, 55, 60, 71, 75, 83, 84, 85, 100, 104, 105, 106, 120, 124, 130, 131, 162, 171
chastity, 34, 164
childhood, 12, 19, 46, 57, 76, 81, 134, 138, 172

children, 9, 12, 13, 14, 15, 16, 17, 24, 25, 27, 39, 47, 49, 50, 56, 58, 62, 64, 66, 71, 78, 80, 81, 82, 83, 84, 85, 86, 95, 110, 112, 130, 133, 134, 137, 140, 141, 145, 148, 151, 171
Childs, Geoffrey S, 169, 172
Christianity, 52, 83, 101, 113, 153, 158, 164, 165, 168, 173, 174
Clark, Liz, 166
cognition
    B cognition, 141, 142
    D cognition, 141
cohabitation, 37
coincidences, 97, 99
commitment, 34, 37, 41
communication, 39, 44, 84, 92, 124
community, 70, 73, 91, 93, 96, 110, 129, 143, 146, 151, 153
compassion, 48, 61, 85, 91, 99, 111, 114, 130, 153
complacency, 111, 145, 153
conceit, 41, 57, 140, 147
concrete thinking, 12
confidence, 24, 41, 54, 80, 100, 115, 134, 137, 138, 139, 140, 141, 142, 143, 144
    over-confidence, 139, 140
conjugial love, 34, 35, 36, 38, 41, 142, 164, 165
conscience, 18, 27, 38, 52, 53, 56, 57, 59, 62, 78, 113, 135, 146, 161, 165, 166
    mistaken, 58, 59
consciousness, 13, 15, 18, 19, 29, 49, 50, 51, 68, 75, 82, 87, 103, 115, 116, 117, 118, 119, 120, 121, 123, 124, 125, 127, 137, 147, 153, 159, 170
    altered states, 119, 121, 124, 159
    collective unconsciousness, 45, 123, 165
    personal unconscious, 45
    unconscious, 10, 23, 25, 45, 56, 57, 120, 121, 124, 134, 152, 159, 166
    waking consciousness, 39, 119
contemplation, 15
contentment, 27, 46, 47, 62, 73, 79, 100, 134, 163
correspondence, 9
counselling, 8, 25, 28, 74, 84, 85, 147
courage, 30, 100, 114, 161
crime, 62, 111, 128, 130
crisis, 23, 30, 47, 112, 140, 145, 146, 149, 150
curiosity, 12, 28, 160

De Charms, George, 164, 168, 172
death, 30, 45, 47, 58, 62, 68, 96, 101, 102, 103,
    104, 105, 106, 107, 108, 109, 110, 117, 119,
    121, 124, 133, 134, 135, 141, 150, 159, 167,
    170, 173
despair, 53, 66, 109, 122, 150, 151, 152, 153,
    154
destruction, 108, 115, 129
disasters, 108, 109, 110, 111, 113, 114
disloyalty, 33
disorders, 8, 99, 116, 117, 167
disposition, 23, 95, 121, 124, 157
divine, 11, 19, 20, 27, 31, 38, 46, 47, 48, 49, 52,
    53, 54, 55, 61, 62, 63, 67, 73, 76, 86, 87, 90,
    91, 94, 98, 99, 100, 114, 115, 121, 130, 143,
    144, 147, 149, 152, 156, 157, 158, 160, 162,
    163, 164, 165, 167, 170, 171
    divine enlightenment, 152
    divine humanity, 48, 49, 158
    divine inspiration, 27, 53, 158
    divine love, 87, 94, 144, 158
    divine power, 91
    divine providence, 98, 99, 100, 121, 170
    divine source, 38, 46, 67
    divine spirit, 48, 76, 114
    divine within, 19, 49
    divine activity, 99
dogmas, 13, 14, 148
Dole, George F, 170
double-aspect terms, 164
doubt, 42, 96, 112, 135, 139, 140
dreams, 10, 45, 52, 103, 118, 119, 120, 173
Duckworth, J, 167, 173
Eckersley, Glennyce, 168, 170
effort, 14, 17, 19, 26, 29, 40, 43, 46, 50, 53, 54,
    60, 65, 73, 77, 78, 89, 91, 93, 97, 139
ego, 51, 64, 84, 86, 166, 167
    ego ideal, 86
    ego-orientated, 51
emotion, 15, 16, 20, 26, 42, 67, 69, 76, 108,
    128
empathy, 43, 48, 104
employment, 53, 73
enlightenment, 14, 16, 86, 100, 157, 164
estrangement, 107, 140, 151
eternal now, 15, 18, 46
ethical principles, 142
excuses, 17, 63, 94, 138, 139, 148
existentialism, 25, 57, 86, 151
expectations, 13, 16, 22, 24, 37, 38, 43, 48, 57,
    62, 73, 81, 84, 88, 115, 131, 137, 138, 146,
    152, 157

failings, 18, 44, 52, 53, 54, 57, 77, 79, 84, 85,
    87, 88, 90, 139, 151
failure, 37, 82, 113, 138, 139, 141, 155
faith, 11, 61, 76, 99, 114, 149, 152, 161, 164,
    165, 174
fallacy, 27, 65
fault, 22, 51, 56, 64, 65, 75, 85, 92, 93, 113
fear, 23, 30, 37, 42, 57, 68, 70, 75, 76, 86, 95,
    96, 101, 107, 108, 118, 125, 129, 140, 141,
    148, 151, 161
feeling, 7, 9, 14, 15, 16, 17, 20, 30, 33, 34, 35,
    36, 38, 39, 40, 42, 43, 44, 46, 50, 54, 55, 56,
    57, 59, 65, 67, 68, 69, 72, 73, 74, 75, 77, 78,
    81, 82, 86, 87, 88, 90, 95, 96, 97, 101, 102,
    105, 107, 108, 111, 114, 119, 122, 123, 124,
    125, 126, 134, 135, 140, 150, 152, 155, 156,
    159, 172
feminism, 35
Fontana, David, 166, 167
forces, 49, 53, 78, 125, 126, 129, 146
    dark force, 151
    life force, 46
forgiveness, 60, 61, 62, 69, 85, 123, 132, 153
Frankl, Victor, 109, 110, 167
freedom, 23, 24, 26, 27, 28, 31, 37, 51, 52, 55,
    66, 100, 125, 126, 127, 152, 153, 156, 164,
    168, 171
Freud, Sigmund, 10, 23, 56, 59, 74, 86, 165,
    166
friends, 9, 14, 15, 18, 22, 42, 43, 45, 48, 49, 51,
    56, 62, 73, 78, 88, 89, 95, 96, 102, 104, 123,
    139, 140, 160
Fromm, Erich, 166, 167
future, 15, 18, 51, 60, 70, 97, 100, 126, 140,
    152, 172
gender, 35, 82
Glasser, William, 164
God, 9, 11, 13, 18, 19, 25, 29, 30, 37, 47, 48,
    49, 52, 53, 54, 59, 60, 61, 62, 79, 83, 85, 86,
    87, 89, 90, 91, 94, 98, 99, 100, 110, 112,
    113, 114, 121, 125, 130, 134, 135, 143, 144,
    147, 148, 149, 152, 153, 157, 158, 161, 162,
    166, 167, 168, 170, 172
Goodridge-Clarke, N, 164, 165, 171
Grange, Alan, 165, 169, 171
greed, 113
grief, 65, 80, 108, 152, 154
guilt, 34, 56, 57, 62, 74, 77, 86, 108, 130, 151
    guilty feeling, 56, 57, 108
    illogical guilt, 56
habits, 7, 11, 29, 50, 51, 57, 77, 82
hallucinations, 116, 117

hands, 8, 9, 14, 17, 20, 21, 26, 29, 48, 51, 52, 53, 64, 82, 86, 90, 99, 128, 155, 156, 158

head, 8, 14, 21, 26, 29, 44, 48, 51, 53, 57, 64, 82, 84, 100, 101, 116, 128, 142, 155, 156, 158, 161, 163

healing, 54, 99, 114, 134, 156

health, 8, 11, 56, 96, 97, 110, 142, 169, 170, 172

heart, 8, 9, 14, 16, 18, 21, 29, 33, 34, 38, 43, 48, 51, 52, 53, 57, 62, 64, 67, 68, 73, 78, 79, 82, 90, 91, 93, 94, 99, 109, 114, 128, 131, 152, 153, 155, 156, 158, 159, 161, 162, 163, 166

heaven, 18, 38, 55, 60, 61, 90, 105, 112, 114, 115, 120, 157, 171, 174

heavenly marriage, 35, 38, 163

heavenly state, 18, 47, 134, 163

help, 7, 8, 13, 15, 22, 25, 28, 29, 30, 38, 40, 41, 44, 48, 49, 50, 51, 54, 57, 61, 62, 65, 66, 67, 70, 71, 74, 75, 78, 79, 86, 88, 89, 90, 91, 95, 97, 100, 102, 117, 126, 128, 137, 138, 142, 145, 150, 152, 160, 162, 174

Henderson, Bruce, 167, 173

higher power, 29, 53, 54, 100, 162

honesty, 25, 114, 129

hope, 7, 11, 27, 49, 57, 60, 62, 66, 76, 79, 88, 109, 114, 115, 121, 126, 132, 134, 148, 149, 152, 153, 155

Hull, R F C, 167

human, 8, 10, 11, 16, 20, 21, 23, 24, 26, 27, 30, 31, 36, 43, 45, 48, 49, 52, 53, 56, 61, 66, 77, 82, 86, 94, 96, 99, 102, 105, 112, 113, 114, 115, 120, 122, 125, 140, 142, 148, 151, 157, 158, 159, 160, 166, 170, 172

human nature, 11, 53

human relationships, 77

human spirit, 8, 10, 105

humanistic, 86

humanity, 45, 49, 83, 93, 112, 143, 157, 170

humility, 87, 145

Husain, Ed, 166

hypnogogic experience, 119

ideals, 27, 33, 35, 36, 47, 70, 86, 96, 111, 129, 141, 142, 146, 151, 156

identity, 30, 81, 172

illumination, 14, 21, 106, 112, 152

illusion, 18, 27, 67, 77, 86, 114, 126, 147, 152, 153, 163

ill-will, 62

imagination, 15, 65, 67, 84, 116, 119

immortality, 70, 105

imperfection, 27, 47, 159

impulse, 10, 52, 54, 56, 57, 60, 61, 62, 83, 125, 126, 133, 134, 150, 151, 157, 159

infancy, 47, 140

infatuation, 33, 38

infidelity, 33, 34, 65, 79

inner, 8, 9, 10, 11, 14, 15, 16, 17, 18, 19, 20, 22, 25, 27, 30, 38, 40, 44, 46, 48, 49, 50, 52, 54, 61, 62, 76, 79, 81, 82, 95, 98, 99, 104, 105, 106, 111, 112, 113, 114, 118, 120, 121, 125, 126, 130, 131, 135, 141, 143, 145, 146, 147, 151, 152, 153, 156, 157, 159, 160, 162, 172, 173

inner conflict, 30, 50, 52

inner freedom, 25, 27, 62, 95, 99

inner liberty, 11

innocent suffering, 114

insecurity, 86, 97

inspiration, 17, 19, 46, 67, 86, 96, 100, 121, 125, 126, 136, 146, 151, 157

integration, 30, 156

intrusive thought, 133, 135

Jainism, 52, 67, 94

James, Leon, 123, 164, 167, 168, 169, 172

James, William, 123, 164, 167, 168, 169, 172

Jesus Christ, 21, 48, 49, 51, 61, 66, 68, 80, 85, 86, 94, 97, 114, 122, 153, 158

job satisfaction, 70

judgment, 15, 60, 131, 166, 168, 171

Jung, Carl Gustav, 14, 45, 74, 97, 113, 123, 165, 166, 167

Kingslake, Brian, 164, 165, 166, 167, 172

Kirven, Robert, 170

knowledge, 12, 13, 37, 42, 50, 51, 57, 76, 77, 120, 135, 148, 158, 160, 161

Lasch, I, 167

loss, 47, 58, 101, 107, 108, 109, 111, 112, 114, 115, 122, 149, 151, 153

love, 12, 13, 20, 25, 33, 34, 35, 36, 38, 40, 41, 47, 49, 54, 55, 58, 61, 62, 63, 64, 66, 71, 78, 79, 81, 83, 85, 86, 90, 94, 95, 96, 100, 101, 102, 106, 107, 114, 129, 141, 143, 144, 149, 152, 157, 158, 162, 164, 166, 170, 171

conjugial love, 34, 35, 36, 38, 41, 142, 164, 165

love of knowledge, 13

mature love, 32, 33, 34

lucid dreams, 119, 121

Maginel, Bob, 164, 167, 168, 172

malice, 61, 62, 78, 92

marriage, 34, 35, 37, 38, 39, 40, 41, 145, 165, 171

Maslow, Abraham, 141, 142, 166

materialism, 125
May, Rollo, 165
meaning, 9, 16, 19, 20, 28, 30, 44, 59, 67, 76, 77, 86, 92, 107, 110, 111, 141, 153, 158, 160, 167, 170, 174
meditation, 15, 19, 58
mediums, 8, 45, 47, 58, 104, 124, 134
Meldrum, Claire, 166
memory, 14, 40, 60, 67, 79, 117, 118, 120, 123, 134
mental illness, 118, 121
mind, 8, 9, 10, 13, 14, 15, 16, 18, 19, 27, 29, 34, 37, 38, 43, 45, 49, 56, 60, 72, 73, 75, 76, 78, 79, 82, 84, 86, 90, 91, 93, 95, 100, 103, 104, 111, 114, 115, 117, 119, 120, 121, 122, 124, 130, 134, 135, 139, 143, 146, 148, 151, 153, 154, 157, 159, 160, 161, 162, 172, 173
mindfulness, 15
Moffat, T, 167, 173
Moody, Raymond Jr, 102, 167
morality, 24, 66, 90, 112, 123, 128, 129, 130, 147
motivation, 46, 59, 61, 141, 158
    deficiency motive, 141
    growth motive, 141, 166
    mixed motives, 59, 145, 162
music, 16, 17, 96, 119, 126, 139, 141
mystic states, 14, 19, 107, 123
mysticism, 20, 143, 171
    mystical presence, 47
    mystical states, 118
myth, 45
narcissism, 59, 78
nature, 10, 14, 20, 21, 22, 24, 29, 34, 44, 47, 49, 70, 72, 74, 77, 82, 83, 86, 102, 105, 114, 118, 119, 120, 136, 140, 151, 157, 162, 166, 167, 171, 172
near death experience, 102, 103, 104, 123, 173
negativity, 78, 81, 114, 138
neurosis, 56, 71, 142
    neurotic guilt, 56
    neurotic striving, 71
obsession, 79, 133, 136, 160
order, 20, 27, 29, 46, 58, 73, 77, 79, 99, 129, 143, 153, 157, 159, 160, 170, 173
orientation, 15, 36, 71, 78, 86, 90, 91, 143, 146
    worldly orientation, 15
original sin, 83
outer, 9, 12, 98, 105, 121, 141, 143, 160
out-of-body experiences, 119
pain, 30, 65, 80, 105, 107, 112, 117, 147, 149, 150, 151

parents, 13, 27, 47, 50, 56, 71, 76, 81, 83, 84, 86, 92, 131, 134, 137, 138, 160
peace, 36, 46, 60, 62, 93, 95, 100, 101, 102, 141, 149, 153, 163
personal, 7, 8, 10, 11, 13, 14, 15, 17, 18, 23, 24, 25, 26, 27, 28, 29, 30, 32, 35, 43, 45, 46, 47, 53, 59, 67, 72, 75, 76, 77, 79, 80, 82, 84, 88, 90, 92, 95, 97, 103, 110, 111, 112, 113, 118, 119, 121, 123, 138, 139, 145, 146, 148, 149, 153, 157, 158, 160, 161, 162, 168, 171, 172, 173, 174
    personal change, 29, 149, 161
    personal development, 8, 11, 23, 24, 29, 30, 32, 80, 121, 168
    personal problems, 8, 27, 95, 160
    personal responsibility, 26, 53
philosophy, 7, 13, 50, 87, 91, 99, 111, 169, 172
physical health, 81, 110
pleasure, 18, 27, 35, 54, 59, 61, 72, 73, 75, 79, 122, 139, 150, 153, 162
Pratt, J B, 123, 168
prayer, 15, 89, 90, 91, 100, 167
pride, 16, 57, 64, 68, 78, 87, 88, 148
privacy, 71
prodigal son, 123
projection, 105, 120, 124, 159
proprium, 67, 68, 77, 164, 166, 167
providence (see divine providence), 99, 170
psychic, 45, 119, 121, 123, 124, 173
psychoanalysis, 23, 27, 57, 120, 165
psychology, 7, 8, 10, 11, 24, 26, 30, 56, 74, 76, 93, 113, 120, 121, 155, 157, 168, 169, 170, 171, 172
    psycho-spiritual, 10, 11, 20, 21, 120, 159, 160, 168, 170, 174
psychotherapy, 7, 8, 11, 23, 25, 26, 28, 29, 74, 75, 78, 80, 89, 93, 97, 112, 135, 150, 156, 161
    psychotherapist, 7, 9, 17, 23, 25, 26, 74, 75, 84
punishment, 49, 56, 59, 113, 129, 130, 152, 168
questions, 9, 12, 13, 14, 15, 16, 17, 20, 32, 118, 141, 172
rationality, 11, 31, 95
reality, 14, 18, 21, 44, 47, 56, 95, 98, 107, 111, 113, 114, 115, 117, 120, 124, 148, 151, 168
reconciliation, 64, 66, 96
reformation, 162
regeneration, 80, 162, 164, 166, 167, 169
religion, 8, 11, 15, 20, 67, 76, 79, 86, 89, 90, 110, 113, 133, 153, 166, 167
    religious attitude, 61, 89, 147

religious orientation, 89
religious people, 48, 53, 83, 90, 91, 158
remains, 46
remnants, 46
repentance, 62, 162, 164, 165, 166
reputation, 129, 140
resentment, 39, 64, 67, 77, 123
resistance, 97, 161
resolve, 7, 29, 30, 52, 62, 67, 88, 146, 161
respect, 17, 18, 34, 57, 76, 85, 87, 90, 94, 129,
    140, 163
responsibility, 23, 26, 28, 30, 39, 46, 58, 60, 67,
    78, 99, 112, 133, 161
restraint, 52, 130
resurrection, 101
retribution, 130
Rhodes, Leon, 167, 173
rôle models, 23, 123, 130
Role models, 48
rôles, 23, 24, 30, 35, 56, 58, 59, 72, 108, 123,
    124, 130, 137, 138, 142, 147, 153, 160
Rose, Frank, 164, 167, 168, 172
Samaritan, 62, 123
Samuels, Andrew, 165, 166
science, 9, 14, 24, 70, 99, 119, 125, 147, 174
scientists, 8, 17, 125
self, 7, 9, 11, 16, 17, 18, 22, 23, 24, 25, 27, 28,
    34, 35, 36, 43, 44, 46, 49, 50, 51, 52, 54, 55,
    56, 59, 60, 61, 62, 67, 68, 69, 71, 72, 74, 75,
    76, 77, 78, 79, 81, 82, 83, 84, 85, 86, 87, 90,
    91, 93, 96, 100, 104, 105, 106, 113, 114,
    119, 120, 123, 124, 130, 131, 132, 137, 138,
    139, 140, 144, 145, 146, 147, 148, 149, 150,
    151, 152, 153, 155, 156, 159, 160, 161, 162,
    163, 165, 166, 167, 168, 171, 172
self-absorption, 78, 86
self-acceptance, 59, 153
self-assessment, 76
self-centredness, 59, 71, 78
self-concern, 34, 68, 69, 79
self-condemnation, 146, 151
self-control, 51
self-doubt, 44, 139, 145
self-esteem, 24, 81, 82, 83, 86
self-examination, 75
self-identity, 78, 86
self-image, 84, 147
self-indulgence, 151
self-insight, 17, 25, 28, 54, 74, 75, 161
self-knowledge, 77, 160
self-love, 52, 55, 59, 69, 78
self-merit, 148

self-orientated, 60, 71, 87, 162, 163
self-perception, 81
self-pity, 68, 72, 123, 139
self-preoccupation, 72
self-righteous, 131, 147, 148
self-satisfying, 147
self-serving, 60, 74, 153
true self, 31, 43, 44
senses, 14, 23, 28, 79, 104, 114, 120, 121, 124,
    143, 157, 160
sex, 32, 33, 34, 35, 36, 74, 82, 129, 133
sexual disorder, 79
sexual fantasy, 33, 151
sexual pleasure, 79
sexual relationship, 11, 32, 34, 35, 37, 40, 111
sexuality, 32, 164, 171
shadow, 150, 166
shame, 57, 130
shock, 65, 108, 111, 112
Shorter, Bani, 165, 166, 167, 173
Sigstedt, Cyriel Odhner, 164, 173
Silverman, Ray, 165, 171
Simpson, J, 117, 121, 168
skills, 137, 138, 142
Smart, Ninian, 166
Socrates, 121
space, 12, 18, 29, 46, 104, 128, 157, 158
spirit, 8, 14, 15, 19, 20, 27, 29, 35, 45, 52, 66, 72,
    76, 83, 85, 86, 90, 93, 99, 102, 103, 104, 105,
    106, 115, 119, 120, 121, 124, 125, 134, 135,
    143, 145, 147, 149, 152, 153, 157, 173, 174
spirit of God, 86, 90
spirit of truth, 29, 52, 83, 145, 149
spirits, 45, 46, 49, 102, 103, 104, 105, 106,
    119, 120, 123, 124, 125, 126, 127, 134, 135,
    136, 151, 152, 159, 168
spiritual world, 45, 103, 104, 105, 106, 120,
    124, 158, 159, 165, 167, 168, 173
spirits, 45, 46, 49, 102, 103, 104, 105, 106,
    119, 120, 123, 124, 125, 126, 127, 134, 135,
    136, 151, 152, 159, 168
    angelic spirits, 106, 115, 133, 134, 151, 152,
    166, 168, 170
    evil spirits, 120, 127, 135, 151, 152
spiritual, 7, 8, 9, 11, 14, 20, 23, 25, 26, 27, 32,
    35, 36, 38, 41, 44, 45, 52, 58, 61, 62, 67, 76,
    80, 86, 87, 90, 93, 94, 95, 96, 99, 103, 104,
    105, 106, 113, 114, 115, 119, 120, 121, 122,
    123, 124, 125, 129, 130, 142, 143, 144, 148,
    150, 151, 152, 153, 156, 158, 159, 160, 161,
    163, 165, 167, 168, 169, 170, 171, 172, 173,
    174

spiritual awareness, 90
spiritual force, 41, 86, 87, 94
spiritual gifts, 61, 62, 99
spiritual growth, 32, 80, 93, 95, 119, 152, 156, 159
spiritual state, 35, 38
spiritual teachings, 8, 20
spiritual temptations, 153, 165, 167
spirituality, 18, 29, 157
spiritual law, 103, 124
Stanley, Michael, 164, 165, 166, 167, 168, 169, 171
state, 7, 9, 18, 19, 25, 34, 35, 37, 38, 40, 46, 47, 52, 60, 62, 65, 68, 74, 75, 76, 78, 79, 84, 86, 87, 90, 91, 93, 97, 100, 101, 102, 103, 104, 106, 108, 110, 111, 112, 114, 115, 117, 118, 119, 120, 121, 122, 123, 124, 126, 128, 130, 134, 145, 146, 148, 149, 151, 152, 153, 154, 159, 162
exalted state, 146
status, 51, 79, 96, 114, 142, 150
struggle, 52, 66, 153, 162
suicidal thoughts, 122
superego, 57, 59
supernatural, 96, 125
support, 40, 49, 58, 59, 110, 150
surrender, 53
suspicion, 30, 56, 77, 92
Suzuki, D T, 166, 172
Swedenborg, Emanuel, 7, 8, 9, 10, 11, 15, 19, 20, 21, 25, 31, 34, 35, 36, 38, 41, 45, 48, 49, 52, 55, 60, 61, 62, 63, 67, 69, 73, 76, 77, 79, 80, 85, 86, 91, 94, 96, 98, 100, 103, 104, 105, 107, 114, 115, 119, 120, 123, 124, 127, 132, 134, 135, 136, 142, 144, 149, 151, 152, 153, 154, 155, 157, 158, 159, 162, 163, 164, 165, 166, 167, 168, 169, 170, 171, 172, 173, 174
synchronicity, 97
Synnesvedt, Sig, 168, 171
Taylor, Eugine, 170
temptation, 52, 53, 54, 60, 61, 165, 167, 169
therapy (see psychotherapy), 7, 8, 23, 25, 26, 28, 74, 75, 78, 80, 89, 97, 112, 150, 156
time, 8, 15, 18, 27, 28, 33, 37, 40, 43, 46, 47, 49, 51, 56, 58, 59, 65, 68, 70, 72, 73, 79, 80, 81, 83, 87, 89, 97, 98, 99, 100, 102, 103, 104, 107, 108, 109, 111, 117, 121, 124, 126, 128, 131, 134, 137, 138, 139, 140, 141, 142, 145, 153, 157, 158, 160, 162, 163
timelessness, 46, 103
Tolstoy, L, 19, 164

trust, 20, 34, 41, 46, 47, 80, 93, 94, 100, 111, 129, 134, 140, 150, 162
truth, 14, 15, 16, 17, 19, 20, 21, 23, 26, 29, 41, 46, 76, 84, 85, 87, 121, 123, 127, 141, 142, 143, 147, 149, 153, 154, 163, 164
Tutu, D, 166
understanding, 9, 12, 13, 14, 16, 17, 19, 27, 30, 41, 43, 46, 49, 54, 64, 78, 93, 113, 121, 125, 131, 142, 143, 155, 157, 158, 160, 161, 162, 163, 170, 171, 174
unhappiness, 7, 62, 122, 123, 134, 152
universal human, 44
unworthiness, 151
use, 9, 14, 16, 26, 28, 50, 51, 64, 72, 73, 74, 76, 89, 93, 101, 109, 119, 123, 129, 142, 166
values, 25, 30, 35, 44, 52, 59, 76, 82, 85, 90, 96, 97, 105, 119, 121, 123, 124, 141, 142, 146, 151, 153, 161, 162
Van Dusen, Wilson, 118, 120, 124, 164, 166, 168, 171, 172, 173
vanity, 59, 147
vastation, 152
vice, 50, 61, 114
virtue, 78
visions, 9, 50, 101, 103, 119, 120, 125, 151, 170, 173
voices, 9, 15, 16, 19, 20, 48, 58, 62, 64, 78, 81, 82, 83, 91, 103, 112, 116, 117, 118, 119, 120, 121, 124, 139, 159
Von der Heydt, V, 168
Wallerstein, J S, 165
Watts, F, 164
well-being, 8, 11, 18, 30, 46, 47, 76, 128, 156
Wilber, Ken, 165
Wilber, Treya, 165
Williams, M, 164
wisdom, 62, 76, 85, 87, 90, 100, 114, 119, 143, 158, 159, 170, 171
Worcester, William L, 164, 172
work, 10, 17, 18, 27, 29, 30, 38, 39, 40, 41, 42, 45, 57, 58, 59, 60, 61, 65, 70, 71, 72, 73, 75, 77, 82, 84, 90, 99, 111, 112, 116, 118, 122, 125, 129, 135, 140, 142, 146, 147, 156, 159, 170, 172, 173
world view, 111
worry, 7, 77, 95, 96, 97, 99, 118, 133, 140
worship, 90, 158, 163
worthiness, 87
wrongdoing, 61, 62, 65, 123, 128, 130, 131, 132
Wunsch, W, 166, 170
zeal, 68, 71